Learning from the Inside-Out

Learning from the Inside-Out

Child Development and School Choice

Manya C. Whitaker, PhD

ROWMAN & LITTLEFIELD
Lanham • Boulder • New York • London

Published by Rowman & Littlefield
A wholly owned subsidary of The Rowman & Littlefield Publishing Group, Inc.
4501 Forbes Boulevard, Suite 200, Lanham, Maryland 20706
www.rowman.com

Unit A, Whitacre Mews, 26–34 Stannary Street, London SE11 4AB

British Library Cataloging in Publication Information Available

Library of Congress Cataloging-in-Publication Data
Names: Whitaker, Manya Catrice, author.
Title: Learning from the inside-out: child development and
school choice / Manya Whitaker.
Description: Lanham, Maryland : Rowman & Littlefield, 2016. |
Includes bibliographical references.
Identifiers: LCCN 2016023507 (print) | LCCN 2016035512 (ebook) |
ISBN 9781475822922 (cloth) | ISBN 9781475822946 (Electronic)
Subjects: LCSH: Individualized instruction. |
Education – Decision making. | Child development.
Classification: LCC LB1031.W485 2016 (print) |
LCC LB1031 (ebook) | DDC 371.39/4–dc23
LC record available at https://lccn.loc.gov/2016023507

∞™ The paper used in this publication meets the minimum requirements of
American National Standard for Information Sciences—Permanence of Paper
for Printed Library Materials, ANSI/NISO Z39.48–1992.

Printed in the United States of America

Contents

Foreword

Parents have many chances to advocate for their children's education. In reading this book, you will learn how to apply core lessons from the science and practice of developmental and educational psychology as you make decisions on supporting your child's positive growth.

Every child has unique educational qualities, but sometimes it is not obvious how to address them. My husband and I have experienced that dilemma many times—where to send our sons to school, how to address a difficulty they had with friends, and how to approach a teacher with whom we had a disagreement. Neither of our sons was a traditional learner.

In fact, there are *no* traditional learners. Nor can any narrowly focused school environment meet every child's needs. That's what this book is about: helping to equip parents to identify and address their child's unique learning needs—that precious personality, individual profile of intellectual assets and limitations, and one-of-a-kind experience in a family, community, and culture.

In *Learning from the Inside-Out: Child Development and School Choice*, Dr. Manya C. Whitaker takes insights from the twin fields of developmental and educational psychology and shares them with parents. The ideas in this book, including different models of education and areas of the child's development, are highly relevant to the needs of parents, who invariably face challenges in making decisions and advocating for their children.

Dr. Whitaker is well qualified to offer this advice. An expert in child development, she has degrees from Dartmouth College and Vanderbilt University and is now teaching at Colorado College. Moreover, Dr. Whitaker has a genuine interest—and considerable talent—in reaching out to families. She has honed her message over several years in consulting with parents. The result before you is a wonderfully accessible book with a clear framework that distills and illustrates research findings about children and implications for education.

Dr. Whitaker believes strongly, as do I, in equity for children. An equitable education means giving children what they need as individuals—possibly a chance to perform in theatrical performances, extra help with mathematics, or a plan for tracking their own on-task behavior. Equity is *not* the same as giving every child the same education. That is a premise of this book. Parents will learn about how to focus on their children's individual needs and determine the right kinds of school environments and services that may be necessary for personal and educational success.

There are no simple recipes for good parenting in this book. That, also, is a core assumption. Knowing your child and matching your child's needs with specific educational resources is not easy. Fortunately, the book itself is written in a warm and encouraging tone, and Dr. Whitaker communicates faith in the abilities of parents to make good choices.

In the book, you will learn about specific types of schools that you might want to consider for your children. You will find that some kinds of environments are better suited than others to children with particular needs. The characteristics of individuals as they progress through the periods of childhood and adolescence are also examined. Finally, you will learn about theoretical perspectives in developmental psychology and how they undergird various instructional practices and styles of relating to children.

Parents today face serious challenges in raising their children, and knowledge of child development won't solve all parenting problems. It did not solve ours. But it can enhance parents' sensitivity to the characteristics of children—to an awareness of their gifts, to an understanding of the hardships they face, and to their changing needs as they grow and change.

I wish you the best as you learn from this book and determine its applications for your child, whether that involves choosing a school or talking with a teacher about a concern. I think you will be grateful that Dr. Whitaker has chosen to share her talents with us all.

Teresa M. McDevitt, PhD
Professor of Psychological Sciences
University of Northern Colorado
Greeley, Colorado

Acknowledgments

This book was not my idea. I owe the conceptualization of this book to my graduate advisor, Kathy Hoover-Dempsey, who showed me the power of informed parents. Her work on family-school partnerships taught me that all parents, no matter their life circumstances, want the best for their children but may not always have access to the information necessary to do the best for their children. This book is my attempt to follow my advisor's lead and equip parents with what they need to do the most difficult job of all.

Through studying the intersection of homes and schools for the past 10 years, I've realized that my own parents did an amazing job at giving me and my brother what we needed to succeed in school. While Clint went off to military school, I stayed home and attended my neighborhood public school. We learned different things that led to different paths, but each of us excelled in our own way because we were in the environment that fit us best.

But it wasn't until I was an undergraduate that I truly felt what it was like to be in a classroom with a teacher who not only cared *about* me, but *for* me. Abigail Baird was my first mentor and is the reason I chose this career path. Though brilliant, it was not her intellect that impressed my 18-year-old self; it was her genuine commitment to her students. She remains my professional inspiration and is the kind of teacher I envision in every classroom I describe in this book.

During graduate school I was fortunate enough to gain another mentor in Rich Milner. He is the reason I chose to apply my psychological training to education. While in his classes I had no idea of the depth of influence he's had on the field of urban education. I am, however, aware of the depth of his influence on me. Rich gave me the best advice you can ever give a teacher: "Meet them where they are, but don't stay there." This mantra shapes my own teaching practices and helped me articulate the message of this book.

Together, these people shaped how I think about parenting, learning, and teaching. Without them, I wouldn't have had the experiences necessary to gain the knowledge I share here. And without my partner, Michael Sawyer, I wouldn't have had the emotional fortitude to see this project through. In the moments when I was too tired or too overwhelmed, he reminded me that this book matters.

I am forever indebted to all of you.

Introduction

It is no surprise that parental conversations about education are most often about which schools are better and which schools will best prepare their child for college. Choosing a school is one of the most important decisions a parent can make. We look at test scores, class sizes, and extracurricular offerings. We visit schools and talk to teachers to see if they are warm and nurturing. We rely on family and friends for recommendations, because if they liked it, we'll like it too, right?

This is not always the best method for evaluating schools. As school districts respond to ever-changing educational policies and standards, the schools that were excellent last year can be terrible this year. The realities of teacher turnover, school closures, funding cuts, and the emergence of charter schools necessitate constant reevaluation of what counts as quality education.

In the private market of public education, schools are competing for students. They market themselves by drowning parents with jargon about college prep, expeditionary learning, and science, technology, engineering, and math (STEM) education. They describe their teachers as highly qualified and their teaching practices as inquiry-based. While more options are always better than too few, parents often find themselves overwhelmed when trying to figure out what all that means and which is "better."

Better! In this book, you'll discover that there really are no such things as "better" schools. Just as schools change every year, so do children. What is better for your son may be worse for your daughter, and what worked last year may not work this year. What matters more than test scores and other commonly cited indicators of a good school is what educational psychologists call the student-school fit.

Student-school fit describes how well a child's needs align with what the school offers. In this book I challenge the idea that kids should adjust to school and instead suggest that kids should be placed in schools where little adjustment is required. What kids are able to do, how they think, and what they're interested in are moving targets that directly relate to their educational achievement. This book is about how changes in your child should affect changes in their schooling. It is about the intersection of child development and learning.

ORGANIZATION

The book is organized to first overview six broad models of schooling. In covering Montessori, Waldorf, and charter schools among others, I offer a historical timeline of how and why certain models of education emerged. Each model is described with respect to its overall educational philosophy, teaching strategies, curriculum, and ideal type of student.

In Part I of the book I review child development, paying close attention to the natural timeline of children's cognitive and social growth. By focusing on temperament and personality, I identify what aspects of development are open to influence and what aspects are just who children are. I dissect the idea of intelligence, what it means, and how parents and teachers affect children's perception of their own intelligence.

I then discuss special developmental considerations such as giftedness, learning disabilities, and other things that may require unique learning accommodations. I end this section by overviewing aspects of development that are often overlooked when it comes to schooling: racial/ethnic identity, multilingualism, and sexual identity development.

Part II of the book is all about education and how people learn. Chapters on Constructivism, Humanism, Socioculturalism, and Behaviorism begin with overviews of the theory, including information about what kind of parental support is required to optimize student achievement. They also contain examples of a public school using this pedagogical method, a discussion of what it looks like in the classroom, and a section on the cognitive and social traits that facilitate academic success within that model.

The final chapter of the book is about diversity. Almost half of US public school students fall under the category of Culturally and Linguistically Diverse (CLD). Because schools often fail to state how they address issues of difference, I offer readers insight into how schools can meet the educational needs of racial/ethnic minorities, nonnative English speakers, and children from low income families.

This book is meant to make school choice easier. Toward that end, all chapters include a vocabulary box that defines key terms and phrases mentioned in the chapter and in larger educational discourse. There are also conclusory "takeaways" that summarize the major points in the chapter for quick reference when you're in the midst of filling out enrollment applications.

My hope is that this book will be a reference guide as you and your family move through children's educational journeys. I want readers to finish this book with a firm understanding of how children develop over time, and of how those changes relate to their academic achievement.

As a developmental educational psychologist, it's easy for me to see when academic failure is not failure at all; it's usually the result of a poor fit between what a child needs and what the school offers. I hope this book makes it easy for you to see the same.

Chapter One

School Choice(s)

Why are there so many different types of schools? What happened to sending your kids to the school down the street?
— Grandmother of three elementary students

A BRIEF HISTORY OF US SCHOOLING

If you've spent any time researching schools, you know there are tons of options available. What you may not know is what distinguishes one school from another. Sure, things like new buildings and *smart classrooms* are attractive, but what about what actually happens in the classroom? Do the school's discipline policies align with the values you want your child to learn? Will the instructional practices engage your child or will your child be bored in class?

The United States once had a single model of schooling. In the eighteenth and nineteenth centuries the one-room schoolhouse was the only way we taught children. Regardless of age, all neighborhood kids were packed into a single room with a single teacher. Students were divided into grades and instructed in the basics of reading, writing, and arithmetic.

War, immigration, and the industrial revolution prompted a shift away from that model and toward more vocational training. Children from affluent families learned the classics and were tracked into professional schools to become doctors and lawyers. Children from working class families rarely received more than an 8th grade education—the basic skills required to work in factories.

The Cold War and the 1957 launch of *Sputnik* prompted the United States to reevaluate its curriculum. To keep from being outpaced by other countries, we shifted from skills training to content acquisition. Thus began our focus on science, technology, engineering, and math (STEM).

Shortly on the heels of such international comparisons came an in-depth investigation of the US school system. Turns out, not only were we not educating children to compete internationally, we were also educating children unequally depending upon social class, location, and race. *The Coleman Report* (1966) brought to light the reality that children from low income and working class families were receiving a subpar education compared to their wealthier peers.

President Lyndon B. Johnson took action and helped pass the *Elementary and Secondary Education Act of 1965*. This extremely long document outlined the quality of education all children were to receive in US public schools. What it did not outline was how children were to receive this education.

You can imagine that at this point parents began to pay closer attention to what was happening in their children's schools. Prior to the 1960s, parents tended to trust that the school was doing what it was supposed to do, and never really considered educational decision-making a "thing" to be concerned about. But after hearing how poorly schools were educating children (especially children from certain demographic groups), parents took a keen interest in where their children went to school.

By the 1970s, the federal government had begun creating national programs designed to boost the academic achievement of underachieving and underserved students. One of the most notable programs is *Head Start*. This program provides free preschool for low income families. Data on the success of Head Start is varied, but what matters more is that it prompted the creation of other targeted educational interventions.

Indeed, we seem to create new schools retroactively instead of pro-actively. Sure, we respond to future labor force needs, but we primarily create schools in response to social comparison. Whether it's international competition or intranational inequities, our impetus for change is strongly rooted in our desire to be the best. The problem is that we aren't really sure how to become the best.

In that confusion, we've devised multiple schooling approaches for improving our education system. Some are based on instructional techniques, others target specific demographic groups, while yet some are in direct response to current political agendas. Their varied emphases on teaching practices, student needs, and macro level social issues can make deciphering between them difficult.

EDUCATIONAL POLICY AND SCHOOL CHOICE

Since the 1970s, the US Department of Education has been deeply invested in creating policies that ensure all children, regardless of race, income, religion, or gender, have the opportunity to attain a high quality education. This has never been truer than it is in today's *age of accountability.*

Accountability is another way to think about who is to blame for academic underachievement. We continue to pass the buck by implementing policies around *school choice* so that when a student doesn't do well in school, whoever chose that school is to blame. While this policy does not solve systemic problems in our educational system, it does encourage families to think critically about where and why they send their children to school.

Educational legislation like *No Child Left Behind* and the *Every Student Succeeds Act* make this decision more difficult because parents have access to individual school performance data. Initiatives like *Race to the Top* have created competition between districts for funding and *Common Core State Standards* have raised educational expectations. With shifting standards and diverse methods of meeting them, it's difficult to separate "the good, the bad, and the ugly."

What's more is that schools are being closed due to teacher shortages, chronic academic failure, and poor schooling conditions. As families move in and out of neighborhoods, they take their property tax money with them. Without tax funds to supplement state budgets, many neighborhood schools don't have the resources to stay open and compete with newer, better funded schools.

Parents are now faced with the reality that all schools are not created equal. Moreover, given the increasing privatization of schools, the variability in school options is at its highest in history. Unfortunately, parents are choosing schools based upon outcome measures such as school test scores and graduation and college placement rates. Instead, parents should evaluate schools by input factors related to types of content, teaching methods, and school climate.

THE OPTIONS

There are six broad schooling options beyond traditional models that are attentive to different aspects of children's development: Montessori, Waldorf, Community, Alternative, Magnet, and Charter. The first two are unique due to their pedagogical approach. The middle two serve a specific demographic of students. The last two have special curricula that shape school functioning.

In this section you will find a brief overview of each schooling option. Later in the book we cover the psychological theories that guide how learning happens in each educational model.

Montessori schools. Montessori education is perhaps one of the most popular pedagogical models in the United States. Created by Maria Montessori in Italy in the early 1900s, Montessori didn't permanently migrate to the United States until the 1960s when we were searching for instructional methods to accommodate a focus on content. Montessori falls under the genre of social constructivism (Chapter 7) due to its emphasis on the process of learning.

True Montessori classrooms are grounded in children's developmental needs, so they are multiaged and activity-based. The presence of multiple age groups capitalizes on children's natural inclination to learn from peers through both imitation and direct instruction. Children have freedom to move around the room, talk, and work individually or in groups. This child-centered approach emphasizes student choice and hands-on learning.

While kids will work together, *cooperative learning* is not a requirement. Montessori is about depth of learning, so if a child is engaged in an activity, they are allowed to work in a manner that suits their learning needs. Children *self-pace* through academic content, meaning children in the same class are likely to have varying levels of competency depending upon the child and their interest in a particular subject matter.

It takes a fairly independent child to do well in a Montessori class. It also helps if the child has a pretty good attention span and is curious by nature. So much of the learning in Montessori classrooms is up to the child that kids who need a lot of direction have a hard time reaping the benefits of learning opportunities. Initiative matters a lot in this model of education.

Classroom discipline leaves something to be desired for parents who value good behavior. Despite a great teacher to student ratio, children can sometimes take advantage of the lax atmosphere. While there are strict guidelines regarding accountability and cleanliness, there are rarely assigned seats, posted rules, or harsh consequences for misbehavior. Disagreements are handled on a case by case basis, with a teacher (called Directors) acting as mediator.

Proponents of Montessori, however, appreciate the creativity and independence it encourages in children. Many students thrive in a classroom where instruction is student-guided instead of teacher-directed. Specially trained teachers are just one component of the teacher-student-environment triangle. The freedom to move around the room at will aligns well with the social needs of all children, especially young children who engage in environmental exploration.

Many graduates of Montessori schools outperform their peers on academic assessments because learning is concept-based, not skills-based. Whereas many students learn long division procedurally, Montessori schools emphasize the reasoning behind mathematical processes. It may take longer for students to acquire content knowledge, but when they do, they've truly learned it; they aren't just memorizing for Friday's test.

Critics of Montessori say it is unrealistic and doesn't prepare children to work well in structured, group-oriented environments. Further, the creation of Common Core State Standards has pushed many Montessori schools to become private in order to implement their unique pedagogy.

Waldorf schools. Borne of humanism (Chapter 8), Waldorf schooling is focused on the whole child. The curriculum is divided into age groups so that it is developmentally appropriate for children in the categories birth–7 years, 7–14 years, and 14–18 years. The Association of Waldorf Schools in North America outlines the three guiding questions in a Waldorf school:

1. How do we establish within each child his or her own high level of academic excellence?
2. How do we call forth enthusiasm for learning and work, a healthy self-awareness, interest and concern for fellow human beings, and a respect for the world?
3. How can we help pupils find meaning in their lives?

Classes in a Waldorf school can be highly artistic and may heavily involve nature. Courses such as painting, cooking, and gardening are not uncommon in a Waldorf school. Art and foreign language are as central to the curriculum as math, writing, and history. Some schools even offer courses on sewing and movement to help children exercise their bodies as well as their brains. In private Waldorf schools, there may be religious elements to the curriculum due to Waldorf's conservative Germanic roots.

Parental engagement is a big part of Waldorf education, as parents are part of the learning community. It is common for parents to volunteer in classes, in the front office, or with community projects. Parents also serve on councils or other forms of governance to help oversee the functioning of the school. At private schools, parents can also influence course offerings and teacher hiring.

Children who thrive in a Waldorf school are kids who are independent, creative, and have high *emotional intelligence*. Positive relationships are at the core of a Waldorf class, so kids who are shy or a bit socially anxious find themselves very comfortable in this setting. Conversely, children who like to be the center of attention, and who can be a bit confrontational, or enjoy a lot of structure, may find it difficult to fit within this chaotic environment.

The transition from a Waldorf school to a traditional school can be difficult. Effective instruction in Waldorf schools incorporates a lot of creativity, which requires resources beyond textbooks and paper. Field trips, projects, and performances are commonplace in Waldorf classes. Teachers integrate technology into almost all core subjects, helping students connect to communities beyond their own.

Like a Montessori curriculum, the Waldorf curriculum is focused on depth. The pacing is therefore slower than in traditional schools and can make it seem as though Waldorf students are not learning. In truth, Waldorf has learning goals beyond traditional academic content; empathy and compassion are expectations in Waldorf schools. In accordance with humanism, emotional well-being is a prerequisite for academic learning.

Despite its popularity, Waldorf schools are not faring well in the cutthroat world of standardized testing. Parents (and politicians) want to see immediate and measurable results. Unfortunately, Waldorf students are not "trained" to sit for hours and take high stakes tests. In fact, the anxiety provoked by such situations is the antithesis of a Waldorf education. Many consider Waldorf to be too soft an approach to educating children in the twenty-first century.

Community schools. Community schools are perhaps the oldest model of education in the United States, though they were not originally called such. Community schools are *full service* schools that work closely with community organizations to provide resources to students and their families. There are approximately 5,000 community schools nationwide that offer comprehensive services to the community, such as after-school programs and summer school, dedicated offices/personnel for parent engagement, and medical, dental, and psychological health facilities.

The Coalition for Community Schools describes community schools as having these attributes:

- *Quality education*: The school has a core instructional program with qualified teachers, a challenging curriculum, and high standards and expectations for students.
- *Youth development*: Students are motivated and engaged in learning—both in school and in community settings, during and after school.
- *Family support*: The basic physical, mental, and emotional health needs of young people and their families are recognized and addressed.

- *Family and community engagement*: There is mutual respect and effective collaboration among parents, families, and school staff.
- *Community development*: Community engagement, together with school efforts, promotes a school climate that is safe, supportive, and respectful and connects students to a broader learning community.

Community schools are attractive because they create a one-stop shop for more than students. They are the hub of a neighborhood, thus giving a collection of strangers a sense of shared space. They are also highly valuable in neighborhoods that have limited access to healthcare, transportation, or even fresh food. The community partnerships cut down on cost and time families must expend to access these resources outside of their community.

What community schools don't have is a special curriculum. However, students who attend these schools instead of their neighborhood schools do have higher reading and math scores, as well as higher attendance and graduation rates. This outcome is likely due to enrichment activities like tutoring and mentoring, as well as access to more reliable healthcare, which has a direct influence on children's engagement in school.

In our age of education reform, community schools are on the rise because they address causes of poor educational outcomes from multiple perspectives. Further, they offer parents a way to feel more involved in an increasingly authoritarian school system. Additionally, community schools have been shown to be especially effective for low income students whose financial circumstances limit access to extracurricular opportunities.

Alternative schools. Alternative schools are public schools that serve students with special life circumstances. Many times, students who attend alternative schools have dropped out or been removed from traditional public schools, so most alternative schools are high schools. Alternative schools offer unique schedules that can accommodate students who need to work, have children, or are interested in special vocational training.

To be clear, alternative schools are not solely for "troubled" youth; they are schools for kids whose life contexts include obstacles that make traditional schools undesirable or impossible. Each student is assigned a counselor who helps design an academic schedule aligned with the student's needs and interests. This means that not all students will have the same schedule. Some students may attend school just three days a week while others attend in mornings only.

Students may return to a traditional school upon recommendation of alternative school staff. Most often, the requirement for returning involves positive behavior, improved grades, and student desire. Remaining students graduate from alternative school with a GED or high school diploma. Because many alternative schools are still focused on college prep and/or vocational training, they often have partnerships with local community colleges.

Similar to community schools, alternative schools also have partnerships with community agencies that provide health services, job training, and even housing programs. Personnel working in alternative schools include social workers and psychologists, in addition to traditional teachers and school counselors.

The curriculum, though tailored for each student, is the traditional curriculum found in public schools. Students often self-pace and engage in textbook-based work in addition to some online components. There are rarely projects or group work because each student is at a different place in their schooling. In more vocational alternative schools, students may be required to complete community service or internship hours as part of their coursework.

Though alternative schools have many negative connotations, they can be an optimal choice for students who need more flexibility in their academic schedule. If a community school is not available, alternative schools often have many of the same resources that can facilitate students' ability to fully engage with coursework. In many instances alternative schools make the difference between a dropout and a graduate.

Magnet schools. Magnet schools arose in the 1990s as an alternative to traditional public schools and represent the beginning of the school choice movement. Magnet schools focus on specific academic disciplines as the core of their curriculum such as STEM, performing arts, or environmental education. Despite their specialties, public magnet schools are members of the local school district just like traditional schools, but they have smaller class sizes, are project-based, and often align with social constructivist (Chapter 7) teaching practices.

Students who attend magnet schools do so because they want to indulge their interest in a specific academic area. Even with the rise of charter schools, magnet schools remain a first choice among parents because they are viewed as prestigious, specialized academies. Whether this reputation is deserved or not is often debated, but what is true is that magnet schools cultivate special skills/talents and can be a gateway to vocational opportunities.

The focus on processing and deep engagement yields learning skills that are good preparation for higher education. Most notably, academic magnet programs like International Baccalaureate (IB) are well known for their college prep curriculum and emphasis on community service. Students who complete IB programs can earn a special IB diploma that is viewed favorably by colleges and universities.

The problem with magnet schools is that they are too popular. This means that entry into such a school involves a lottery system in addition to an extensive application process. If you are lucky enough for your name to be drawn, you will need to provide transportation to and from the school if the school is out of your district. This can be unrealistic for parents who work full-time jobs or are otherwise unable to work around the school schedule.

Magnet schools remain a popular option because their academic specialties make parents feel as if they are truly choosing something different. The traditional curriculum aligns with Common Core State Standards and high stakes testing, so parents feel confident in the academic outcomes. The blend of traditional and creative makes magnet schools a good alternative to charter schools, which can be more restrictive.

Charter schools. Perhaps the most politically contentious school at present is the charter school. Contrary to popular belief, charter schools are public schools that supplement public funds with money from private sector businesses. A discussion about the pros and cons of partnering with private corporations is beyond the scope of this book. What is important to note is that private donors can have considerable influence on teacher hiring and curricular decisions.

Charter schools differ from traditional public schools in another major way: they pretty much make their own rules. While charter schools must adhere to state policies regarding testing, they are special because they write their own *charter* which outlines specific guidelines related to recruitment and enrollment, teacher hiring and training, and community partnerships. Everything is covered down to small details like the school calendar, dress code, and disciplinary policies.

Enrolling in a charter school usually involves an application and a lottery. What makes this process unique, however, is that some charter schools are allowed to accept and reject students at will, including special education students. Some charter schools have admissions testing or even interviews to help ascertain student-school fit. In a traditional public school this would be illegal, but a charter school admits students who align with their target demographic.

The student-school fit matters because charter schools offer a variety of programmatic foci. Some charter schools are college prep while others focus on fine arts. What is interesting is that a school can be both a charter school and a Montessori or Waldorf school. The word "charter" does not say much about the curriculum or pedagogical approach; it merely describes the ways in which the school is funded and governed.

Recently, there have been concerns that charter schools are (a) not fulfilling their promises and (b) have even more rules than traditional public schools. The college preparatory charter schools receive a lot of criticism because their test scores are not consistently better than those found in traditional schools. Further, there are some who claim charter schools have lower expectations in order to inflate overall achievement.

To complicate this matter is the reality that charter schools' teacher hiring practices are dictated by their specific charter. What that means is that charters decide what qualifications teachers should have and design their own method of recruiting those teachers. This has resulted in a clear distinction in teaching experience between teachers at charter schools and those at traditional schools.

Charter schools are more likely to hire novice teachers without specialized training. Some say this is because new teachers are cheaper. Others say it's because they are a blank slate for school-specific training. Most believe it is an issue of availability. Charter schools emerge quickly and grow one grade level per year. There just aren't enough highly qualified teachers to fill every classroom in every charter school.

Such a large percentage of inexperienced teachers means there are a lot of issues with classroom management. Many charter schools implement zero tolerance policies for misbehavior. Most charter school students wear a uniform, walk single file with their hands behind their back, and are completely silent during academic instruction. This level of structure makes some parents feel as if their children are being treated as prisoners instead of students.

Conversely, many parents believe in the value of developing positive learning behaviors and aren't bothered by the rule-heavy environment. In fact, these parents support the creation of a structured learning environment that minimizes distractions. Further, proponents of charter schools point to their financial resources and innovative programs as reasons why they prefer charter schools over traditional public schools.

The flexibility in spending practices allows charter schools to take students on field trips, provide enrichment courses like music, PE, or art, and to offer supplemental learning opportunities like after-school tutoring. Many charters have extended school days and school years. Students receive more hours of instruction, often in smaller classes, in classrooms with advanced technology.

College prep charter schools spend a good portion of their budget arranging college visits, hosting workshops on financial aid for families, and providing free SAT and ACT prep. The provision of these opportunities and resources is amazing, but what makes it better is that they start this in 6th grade. Students receive continual information and support from 6th through 12th grade to make college access a reality.

In essence, charter schools offer many of the opportunities all public schools once offered. It is unsurprising then that many parents choose charter schools as a way to provide their children with a well-rounded educational experience, unlimited by financial constraints. Whether you agree with the politics behind charter schools or not, they remain a solid and plentiful option for academic support and extracurricular enrichment.

TAKEAWAYS

There are dozens of schooling options out there. Each school is unique in its own way and offers something for someone. We are quick to make up our minds about a certain type of school based upon things we heard on the news or in line at the grocery store. While there is something to be said for schools that get the popular vote, that doesn't mean a different type of school won't be popular in your household.

For those who aren't in the business and don't eat, breathe, and sleep education, it can be hard to weed through opinions and find facts. The fact is that every school has a purpose and that purpose emerges in different ways. For some schools, the emphasis is on the pedagogy. For others, the core of learning revolves around interpersonal relationships. More recently, schools began to be designed in response to the social and economic needs of a struggling school system.

The impetus for a school's creation is less important than its ability to meet its intended goal. This can be especially difficult for schools designed in a less contentious political climate whose purposes no longer align with our most pressing social issues. They struggle to honor their identity while remaining relevant and desirable in our outcomes-based world.

Despite their emphasis on process, Montessori and Waldorf educations certainly have a place in our schooling community and continue to meet the needs of thousands of students each year. Children who like to take their time, think things through, and express themselves in unique ways find success in Montessori and Waldorf schools.

Children who experience obstacles to learning find support in community schools and alternative schools. Too often we are concerned about academic outcomes instead of focusing on the causes of academic performance. Community schools and alternative schools take a step back and refocus our lens on the physical, mental, and social needs of children.

Magnet schools and charter schools are solution-oriented. Both of these frameworks emerged because we realized we weren't doing

Table 1.1

	Montessori schools	Waldorf schools	Community schools	Alternative schools	Magnet schools	Charter schools
Unique factor	Pedagogy	Pedagogy	Student demographic	Student demographic	Curriculum	Curriculum
Pedagogical model	Constructivism	Humanism	Socioculturalism	Behaviorism	Constructivism	Behaviorism
Upsides	Concept-based, Self-paced	Interdisciplinary, Emphasis on emotional intelligence	Extensive support services	Flexible	Positive reputation, Students can explore interests	Extends schooling options, Focus on achievement
Downsides	Too individual	Too flexible	Rare and time intensive to start	Bad reputation	Hard to get into	Hard to get into, Too strict

something right. Our response was to do a lot of different things in hopes that one of them worked. We didn't count on all of them working for someone. It can be tricky wading through the various types of magnet and charter schools to find the perfect combination of curricular and cocurricular offerings.

Indeed, these two approaches offer parents the most choice, but they are also less standardized and less predictable. Still, if you're willing to put in the legwork, there are magnet and charter schools doing amazing things for amazing students. Just be sure to read the fine print on the applications to ensure the school structure and policies align with your child's interests and needs.

REFERENCES

American Montessori Society. (2015). Retrieved from: https://amshq.org/Montessori-Education/Introduction-to-Montessori

Association of Waldorf Schools in North America. (2015). Retrieved from: http://www.whywaldorfworks.org/02_W_Education/index.asp

Coalition for Community Schools. (2009). *Community Schools Research Brief '09*. Retrieved from: http://www.communityschools.org/assets/1/AssetManager/Community%20School%20Results%202013.pdf

Coleman, J. S., Campbell, E. Q., Hobson, C. J., McPartland, F., Mood, A. M., Weinfeld, F. D., et al. (1966). *Equality of educational opportunity*. Washington, DC: US Government Printing Office.

Institute for Educational Leadership. (2015). *Coalition for Community Schools*. Retrieved from: http://www.communityschools.org/

National Center for Community School. (2015). Retrieved from: http://nationalcenterforcommunityschools.childrensaidsociety.org/

US Department of Education. (2010). National Center for Educational Statistics. *Alternative schools and programs for public school students at-risk of educational failure: 2007–08*. Retrieved from: http://nces.ed.gov/pubs2010/2010026.pdf

———. (2015). Retrieved from: http://www2.ed.gov/about/overview/mission/mission.html

Vocabulary to Know

Associated Words/Phrases	Definition
Smart classrooms	Classrooms with touch-screen boards, projectors, and computers
STEM	Acronym for science, technology, engineering and math
The Coleman Report	A 1966 comprehensive report on U.S. public schools that highlighted unequal educational opportunities across demographic groups
Elementary and Secondary Education Act	1965 legislation that completely rewrote federal public school laws. Most known for its direct handling of discriminatory practices and as the predecessor to the No Child Left Behind Act of 2001
Head Start	A federally funded preschool program for low income students
Age of Accountability	A phrase describing the importance of high test scores
School choice	A policy in which parents/families are able to send their children to a school of their choosing
No Child Left Behind	The 2001 reauthorization of the Elementary and Secondary Education Act. It focused on improving student achievement by holding teachers and schools accountable for high test scores
Every Student Succeeds Act	The 2015 reauthorization of the Elementary and Secondary Education Act. It reduced the heavy reliance on test scores as a way to evaluate teacher quality. It also encouraged a reduction of standardized testing
Race to the Top	A federal educational grant program intended to help schools improve the quality of their teachers, teaching practices, and curriculum
Common Core State Standards	National K-12 educational standards intended to universalize student learning outcomes
School climate	The social and emotional "feel" of a school
Cooperative learning	An instructional strategy in which small groups of students of varying academic levels work together to deepen their learning
Self-pacing	When a student directs the speed at which they move through the curriculum
Emotional intelligence	The ability to identify and manage your own and others' emotions
Full service school	A school that integrates academic learning with physical, mental and social services for the entire community
International Baccalaureate	An international curriculum focused on intellectual, social, emotional and personal skill development
Charter	A document in which a charter school's rules and bylaws are carefully outlined
Highly qualified teacher	As stated in No Child Left Behind, a teacher who: • Hold at least a bachelor degree from a four-year institution • Fully <u>certificated</u> or licensed by the state • Demonstrates competence in each <u>core academic subject area</u> in which the teacher teaches

Figure 1.1

Part I

CHILD DEVELOPMENT

In Part I, I focus on child development. "Development" includes kids' physical, cognitive, and social growth. Content in each chapter in this part is grounded in developmental theories from famous psychologists like Jean Piaget, Lev Vygotsky, Carol Dweck, Albert Bandura, Ivan Pavlov, and B. F. Skinner. Theories of development are derived from dozens, sometimes hundreds, of studies of children around the world. The results from each study are combined to create a theory about how children develop *in general*.

Because development is a function of both genetics (nature) and environment (nurture), not everything will be applicable to every child. Don't worry if psychological theories state that 2-year-olds should speak 50–75 words and your child knows only 30 words. Language development, like all aspects of development, is heavily influenced by dozens of factors. What matters more is that you are aware of what your child can do at any given time.

Children's capabilities are not always indicative of their potential. In other words, what a child can do is not necessarily predictive of what they will be able to do in the future. For example, a child with slow language development does not mean they will struggle with reading or writing. It may be that they are waiting for a reason to talk, and once they start school you will be more worried about how to get them to stop talking.

What children can do *now* is indicative of how their brains are working *now*. It's incredibly important that parents and families are aware of children's abilities so they can make developmentally appropriate decisions about their education. It is equally as important to adjust kids' educational experiences as they reach developmental milestones.

By the end of Part I you will know how the brain works and how brain development is influenced by environmental factors. You will also have a good sense of what to expect in your child's development from birth through adolescence. I help clarify complicated issues like learning styles, intelligence, and motivation by revealing how they are a result of both natural brain processing and educational experiences. With a firm ability to evaluate your child's academic and social capabilities, you will be ready to take on Part II: How People Learn.

Chapter Two

The Intersection of Development and Learning

I was just going with the flow, never really thinking about development. I just expected it to happen.

—Mother of two high schoolers

DEVELOPMENTAL PSYCHOLOGY

Developmental psychologists are concerned with the physical, cognitive, and social growth of children from birth through adulthood. Three questions guide developmental research:

- *Continuity*—Is development a gradual process of change, or is it punctuated by periods of rapid change and the sudden emergence of new forms of thought and behavior?
- *Sources of development*—What are the contributions of genetic heredity, the environment, and culture to the process of developmental change?
- *Individual differences*—How does a person come to have stable individual characteristics that make them different from all other people?

The first two questions have been well answered through decades of psychological research. The final question about individual differences is often studied by developmental and social psychologists who are interested in the influence of social factors like culture on children's development. Some things like understanding facial expressions and the development of language have been found to be universal developmental milestones.

21

Other things like gender identity and emotion regulation are dictated by the mechanics of language. For example, many Native American tribes do not have words for "male" and "female," thus changing how children view their own identity. In Sanskrit there are dozens of words for "love," so it makes sense that Hindu Indian children exhibit prosocial behaviors sooner than Christian US children. The amount of influence culture has on development is still under study.

But for now, psychologists do agree on when to study development. To get a clear picture of what happens developmentally, when it happens, and why it happens, psychologists study children in developmental stages. All this means is that children are divided into age groups based on what their bodies and brains are doing at a particular time. Most developmental research on children divides kids into six stages:

1. Infancy (birth–2 years)
2. Early childhood (2–6 years)
3. Middle childhood (6–10/11 years)
4. Early adolescence (10/11–14 years)
5. Adolescence (14–16 years)
6. Late adolescence (16–19 years)

These numbers continue to change because some aspects of development are happening earlier now than they have happened in prior generations. For example, puberty in girls once started, on average, around age 14. Today most young girls begin puberty closer to age 11 and, for some, as young as 8. As we learn more about what triggers the onset of puberty and developmental shifts in general, these developmental stages may change to facilitate more accurate research.

In general, however, the field of psychology agrees on these age-groups and on the developmental milestones that happen within each range. Developmentalists are particularly interested in the changes that mark advancements in what children can do, how children think, and how they interact with others. This chapter overviews the physical, cognitive, and social changes that happen during each stage of development.

Infancy. If infancy had a theme, it would be "so much, so fast." The period from birth through 2 years is marked by an emerging sense of self and all of the beautiful (and sometimes frustrating) experiences that come with a baby's budding knowledge of who they are and where they fit in the world.

Babies' brains are always growing by creating and refining neuronal connections. The more neurons in the brain, the more pathways there are between different parts of the brain. Consequently, babies think about things faster because their brain lobes are starting to work together to process information. In addition to faster *processing speed*, infants are beginning to develop memory systems and will also exhibit *goal-directed behavior*.

Unsurprising to anyone who has worked with very young children, neuronal growth in infants is focused heavily in parts of the brain related to language development. The progression from incomprehensible gurgling to phonemic babbling to effective language use happens within the first two years. By age 2, children can speak about 50–75 words and can understand approximately 200 words.

What young children say suggests something else about what is beginning to happen in their development: a sense of self is emerging. Many children's first words are self-oriented, meaning they are words that are important to the child. Sometimes it's their own name, but more often it's the name of their favorite toy or object or person.

If we pay close enough attention to what words are said to whom and when, we can catch glimpses of kids' unique personalities. A 1-year-old who uses the remote control to feed her stuffed gorilla is not only demonstrating her capacity for symbolic and imitative play, but also her emotional growth.

Between birth and 2 years, infants create bonds with caregivers and even bonds with toys. We see this play out when we take our children to day care or when we accidently leave a favorite stuffed animal at home. Some kids handle separation from the familiar fairly well and can be easily persuaded that everything is okay. Other children cry and scream at the thought of being separated from what has always brought them comfort.

These types of *attachments* begin to develop at 6 or 7 months of age. Why some kids handle separation better than others is not fully understood just yet, but we are fairly certain it has a lot to do with a child's ability to regulate their emotions. Children with *temperaments* (Chapter 3) that lean toward the curious and energetic tend to have an easier time leaving their caregiver. Children with low thresholds for arousal will likely have separation anxiety.

All types of reactions to separation are your child's attempts to regulate their emotional response to a new environment with new objects and new people. By age 3 or 4, children are able to self-soothe enough to be away from their caregivers and benefit from exposure to newness. The more children interact with the world, the faster they develop the capacity to manage their world.

So even if your child is a screamer at the gates of day care, take solace in the fact that there is much more happening than meets the eye. Infancy is

Table 2.1 Major milestones in infancy

Physical development	Cognitive development	Social development
Prefrontal cortex and language areas	Intentional and goal-directed behavior	Emotion regulation
Creation and refinement of neuronal pathways	Emergence of object permanence	Attachment to caregivers
Most brain structures present by 2 years	Cause and effect relationships	Language comprehension
Gross motor skills (e.g., crawling, walking)	Categorization	Self-recognition
Fine motor skills (e.g., reaching, grasping)	Sustained attention	Symbolic play
	Improved memory	Imitation
	Faster processing speed	

one of two periods where we see the fastest physical and cognitive development. While every child develops at their own rate, you can be fairly certain that by age 2 your child is fully prepared to take on the social and emotional challenges that mark early childhood and the transition to school.

Early childhood. The theme for early childhood is "sophistication." Development slows greatly during ages 2–6 years, but there is still a lot going on, especially in the brain. The cognitive skills that developed during infancy are becoming much more sophisticated during early childhood. Kids are now able to comprehend a lot of information, make sense of it themselves, and express their ideas in a nuanced fashion.

Young children are also starting to experiment with abstract mental functions like inductive and deductive reasoning. While 6-year-olds can't quite solve complex problems, they do have mastery over the concepts of "same" and "different," and are beginning to understand patterns. Socially, kids in early childhood can now see how people can be the same in some ways and different in others.

For example, early childhood is when children adopt cultural gender norms. Girls want to be princesses, wear pink, and play with baby dolls. Boys want to be athletes, play with trucks, and roughhouse with one another. Even though they have the same parents, girl-boy siblings see themselves very differently. Children adopt behaviors they see same-sex people exhibiting.

Mom is a girl, I am a girl. Mom wears dresses, I wear dresses. Dad is a boy, I am a boy. Dad shaves, I shave. This restrictive linear thinking can cause problems when children see a girl wearing blue or a boy with long hair. Three-year-olds confuse appearance and reality. To them, what you see is what you get.

This holds true with judgment as well. Moral reasoning emerges in early childhood. A 4-year-old judges right and wrong based upon the outcome, not the intention, of a behavior. Someone who accidently spills a glass of milk is "badder" than someone who intentionally throws an empty glass on the floor. This type of logic is developmentally appropriate but can be frustrating for parents figuring out the best way to discipline their children.

But fear not! Children in this age group don't behave completely irrationally. Their frontal lobes are just starting to develop, so planning and behavioral regulation are in their early stages, but they are present. Five-year-olds do have reasons for their behaviors, though they may not be able to express them clearly.

The nuances involved in interpreting and expressing emotion are slightly out of reach for such young children. Their frustration at not being able to communicate their desires as clearly as they feel them often emerges in temper tantrums. Similarly, their confusion when a sibling or friend is upset with them for taking a toy is genuine. While they can certainly understand their own emotions, it is much harder for young children to understand others' emotions.

Early childhood has a pretty bad reputation (for example, the "Terrible Twos"), but that's because adults and children are not speaking the same language at this point in development. For kids, it's all about them, while adults are doing their best to teach children how to be considerate of others. If parents can figure out how to ensure things make sense to an egocentric 4-year-old, life will go much smoother than it does when trying to ask a child to behave in a way their brains aren't quite able to facilitate just yet.

Middle childhood. During middle childhood, however, parental expectations of children become much more aligned with their developmental capacities. Kids in the ages of 6 to 10 are the calm before the storm. This prepubescent age range has a theme of "self in context," because now the environment influences development just as much as development influences a child's environment. Most notably, school has a large impact on cognitive and social development.

Children in middle childhood are really just beginning their educational careers. The structure of the learning environment is critical to the specific skills children will cultivate. While a lot of development is spontaneous, some aspects take intentional nurturing to reach their potential. This is especially true of cognitive and social skill development.

Table 2.2 Major milestones in early childhood

Physical development	Cognitive development	Social development
Growth rate slows	Cognitive planning	Adopt gender norms
	Confuse appearance and reality	Morality based on behavioral outcomes
Brain is 90% of full weight	Memory processes advance	Empathy and sympathy emerge
Gross motor skills advance	Information-processing faster and more accurate	Emotion regulation advances
Fine motor skills advance (e.g., coloring, pouring, buttoning)	Egocentric	Physical aggression
	Language skills advance	Emergence of ethnic identity

Piaget called this period of cognitive development, concrete operations. Here is when children move from exploring their environments to intentionally interacting with their environments. Children in this stage of development need hands-on experiences to facilitate the development of neural pathways between different parts of the brain. These new connections allow children to think more abstractly about objects and people.

Now, an 8-year-old understands that just because you change the appearance of an object, the object itself does not change. Piaget believed that such realizations would not arise without a child experimenting with different objects. This is why many elementary classrooms use manipulatives to help explain academic concepts. Most math lessons in the primary grades are accompanied by some physical object (pennies, cubes) to help children "see" abstract relationships between number symbols and values.

Instructions in literacy-based activities become much more student-oriented. Instead of a teacher reading to the class or giving direct instruction, students are given some choice about what to read and write. The provision of choice is the school's attempt to honor a new developmental milestone: individualism. Whereas kindergartners are happy to engage in whole-class learning, older students need time to pause, reflect, and think on their own.

This is because children in middle childhood have a lot of variation in how they think at any given time. How Mary solves two-digit addition on Monday could be completely different from the strategy she uses on the test on Friday. The books Joseph reads in September may not be challenging enough by October. Around age 7 or 8 we start to see giant jumps in how kids think and, consequently, in their academic achievement.

Between grades 2 and 3, or in some states, grades 3 and 4, there is a huge increase in the rigor of schooling. The common saying is that children go from "learning to read" to "reading to learn." The curriculum gets much harder because 8- and 9-year-old children have entered a new phase of cognitive development and can handle difficult work that asks them to combine content and skills in ways that reflect their unique thinking.

A similar shift in social skills occurs during elementary school. Kids in middle childhood are becoming social beings with social identities. Because children can now hierarchically categorize information, they have preferences about everything. They have a favorite color, favorite TV show, favorite toy, favorite teacher, and, most of all, a best friend. Peer groups have structure and intention. Friends are chosen based upon shared interest instead of proximity.

More so now than in early childhood, friend groups are single-sex and display increased command of gender norms. There is a good chance that Lilly's seventh birthday party will involve some type of princess theme and have only girls on the invite list. Howard's seventh birthday is likely to be themed after an action figure and will certainly be boys only.

Children's need for categorization is reflected in the structure and functioning of schooling. Often, teachers have students line up by gender, eye color, or by height. Group work is almost always single-sexed. Many assignments are focused on highlighting the differences that exist within the classroom. Students are encouraged to identify what is unique about their family or themselves in an effort to capitalize on their developing self-concept.

While many parents take issue with teachers putting such a heavy emphasis on children's differences, research suggests there are no negative consequences. In fact, these practices are associated with increased positive behavior and increased student engagement. When done well, teachers incorporate students' interest in categorization into classroom learning. Educators call these "teachable moments." Psychologists call this "developmentally appropriate teaching."

The trick for teachers and parents is to recognize what is appropriate for a particular child, given varying rates of development in young children. There is never going to be a perfect classroom or a perfect teacher who meets all of your child's developmental needs 100% of the time. The best we can hope for is a schooling experience that honors students' developmental needs by making the most of what they can do, while pushing them to do more.

Table 2.3 Major milestones in middle childhood

Physical development	Cognitive development	Social development
Increased muscle mass	Attention capacity increases	Gender norms increase
Increased fat tissue, especially in girls	Need hands-on learning	Individualism emerges
Synaptic pruning in frontal cortex	Categorization and sorting become a strength	Morality based on social relationships
Sex differences in gross motor skills (boys get stronger, girls get agile)	Egocentrism leaves	Social comparison
	Memory strategies emerge	Single-sex friend groups
		Friends based on similarities
		Rule-based play
		Verbal aggression
		Increased self-awareness

Adolescence. Every parent's favorite developmental stage. Psychologists call this period "storm and stress." Parents call it "please just let me survive." For both teens and parents, adolescence is a tough time in life. It is the perfect storm of developmental change.

Part one is physical. Puberty starts in early adolescence, resulting in hormonal shifts that facilitate sporadic growth spurts. Girls tend to have one massive growth spurt whereas boys grow at a steadier pace across a few years. Both sexes have increased body hair and increased muscle mass, but girls also get more fatty tissue. More noticeably, girls develop breasts and boys get facial hair and deeper voices.

These are all the ingredients necessary to facilitate massive change in part two of adolescence: social development. Most important in adolescence is the emergence of *social selves*. In early adolescence, teens have two or three close friends comprising a clique. By age 14, however, adolescents start to move in *crowds* based upon the teams and clubs of which they are a part.

The idea of having multiple identities sounds oddly like a mental illness, but in fact it serves a positive function in adolescence. It allows teenagers to explore different identities while they search for their *ideal self*—the person they want to be when they grow up. By the end of adolescence, teens start to settle into the adult they will become.

But despite conscious planning around their own adulthood, teens have a tough time negotiating relationships with adults in their lives. Conflict between adults and teens is inevitable. Adolescence is when kids seek independence and agency, especially in their personal lives. They are discovering who they are as a person separate from their family, and they need the space to engage in such meaningful exploration.

This exploration includes ethnic/racial identity development as well as sexual identity development (Chapter 6). As scary as this is for parents to contemplate, research shows that when parents trust their teenagers and discuss rules and consequences for behavior, teens are less likely to misbehave and less likely to lie about their behavior. This is good news because their new social savviness means teens can be extremely good liars.

Especially in girls, part three of the storm is cognitive development. There is some truth to the saying that girls develop faster than boys. Neuroscience research tells us that girls' frontal lobes develop before boys', resulting in more sophisticated cognition related to judgment, decision-making, and planning. One hypothesis for why girls are cognitively ahead of boys is because of early onset puberty. Hormonal shifts spark the brain's second attempt to reboot itself.

The mass reorganization of neural pathways means that girls' brains can think faster and more efficiently than boys' brains. It also means that at times a teenager's brain goes offline, resulting in literally thoughtless decision-making. It follows then that girls, because their brains are doing this first, engage in much of their misbehavior during middle school whereas boys tend to get in trouble in high school.

Despite the negative connotations associated with adolescence, it really is a period of beautiful development. The intersection of physical, cognitive, and social growth make adolescence the most vulnerable time in a child's development. For parents and teachers, this means you get more bang for your buck. So while it is most difficult to raise and teach teenagers, it can also be the most rewarding.

Table 2.4 Major milestones in adolescence

Physical development	Cognitive development	Social development
Rapid growth in height and weight	Brain reorganization	Risk-taking increases
Boys have increased muscle tissue	Reasoning skills emerge	Focus on future self
Girls have increased muscle tissue and body fat	Improvement in planning and judgment	Relational aggression in girls
Increased hormones	Increased decision-making skills	Physical aggression in boys
Development of frontal lobe		Multiple friend groups
		Racial and sexual identity develop

EDUCATIONAL PSYCHOLOGY

Educational psychology is the theoretical link between developmental psychology and education. The goal of educational psychology is to understand why some children do really well in school and others do not. Educational psychological researchers study learning from Pre-K through college both in traditional schools and in informal educational settings like museums and, most recently, online classrooms.

Unlike developmental psychological research, educational psychological research is conducted by a range of scholars with varying expertise. Most often, teams of researchers enter schools to better understand a single question: how do people learn? We answer this question from a cognitive, brain-based perspective and from a behavioral perspective—both of which are used to analyze the process of learning throughout this book.

The cognitive perspective is most concerned with changes in the brain that affect the reception, processing, and expression of information. Cognitive psychologists study what people's brains do with educational content, not the content itself. Some of the most pertinent topics studied from the cognitive perspective are brain capacity (how much information can we learn?), memory (how do we store information?), and brain differences (*learning styles* and *learning disabilities*).

The behaviorist perspective is concerned with people's decisions about their actions. Most notably, behaviorism is known for producing research on *operant conditioning* and *classical conditioning* (Chapter 10). In educational psychology, we study behavioral factors that facilitate or impede learning, such as self-regulatory learning strategies, classroom management, and teaching methods.

The social environment in schools offers researchers a lot of additional factors to consider when studying how learning occurs. The most popular topics include motivation, student-teacher relationships, and student diversity. Of course, larger issues related to policies, school funding, and teacher quality affect learning processes, but these topics are more often studied by sociologists, economists, and people with a background in education, not in psychology.

Development and learning. The most well studied topic in educational psychology is the relationship between development and learning. The connection between the two is so tight that the latter cannot be studied without also studying the former. What presents a hiccup for researchers is the nature of the relationship between the two. In fact, there are five hypotheses about how development and learning relate to one another:

1. Development precedes learning
2. Learning precedes development
3. Development is learning
4. Development and learning happen simultaneously, but at different rates
5. Development and learning function cyclically

It is less important whether you believe it is the chicken or the egg than if you acknowledge that both development and learning are vital to children's educational outcomes. Despite agreement that both are important, many cognitive psychologists endorse Piaget's theory of development leading to learning because brain functioning forms the basis for learning processes.

Brain development has implications for how we process information. *Receptive, procedural*, and *expressive skills* "live" in different parts of the brain. The *temporal lobe* is associated with receptive language, the *parietal lobe* is responsible for reading, and the *cerebellum* controls muscle coordination. Damage or underdevelopment in any of those areas can result in learning difficulties.

Similarly, different rates of development in different areas of the brain can contribute to children's learning preferences. The *occipital lobe*—the visual processing center—is the first area of the brain to prune neural connections and is the most developed brain area in young children. Preschoolers are therefore best able to process information visually. This is why children's books are heavy on pictures and short on words.

Continual growth and refinement in the temporal lobe can account for vastly different capabilities between childhood and adolescence. Research on memory suggests that young children can hold, on average, up to five digits in their working memory whereas adolescents can hold up to nine. This makes sense because the *hippocampus*, which is responsible for memory, is housed within the slow-developing temporal lobe.

Finally, the *frontal lobe* is perhaps the most researched area of the brain, especially in adolescents. This part of the brain is the "executive control" and monitors complex processes like problem-solving, decision-making, and judgment. Neuroscience tells us that the frontal lobe is not fully developed until our 30s. Without that part of the brain working at full capacity, children and teens struggle with academic behaviors related to organization and goal-setting, and even classroom behaviors such as impulse control.

Learning—defined as content and skill acquisition—is no less important to educational outcomes than development. After all, the way we measure academic achievement in the United States is based almost solely on students' ability to demonstrate what they know and what they can do.

Vygotsky's theory of the *zone of proximal development* convinced us that information and skills we currently possess are the gateway to new content and skills.

For example, a 4-year-old with a broad vocabulary (content) can understand adult language, comprehend advanced children's books, and has, overall, better capabilities to learn than a 4-year-old with limited vocabulary. A strong vocabulary serves as a guide to help contextualize unfamiliar words. Cognitive psychologists call these guides "schemata." Schemata are used to help make sense of new information.

A major aspect of Piaget's cognitive developmental theory is related to how people use schemata to process information. He called these uses *assimilation* and *accommodation*. If we encounter something new that is closely related to something we already know, we assimilate that information into our existing file, or schema. If we encounter something unrelated to an existing mental file, we accommodate that new information by creating a new mental file.

A good example of these processes is when kids learn about animals. Most preschool-aged kids are familiar with cats and dogs and have separate schema for each. But toddlers may not yet know the difference between the two and might overextend their understandings of dogs to all four legged, furry animals. This is because their limited exposure and vocabulary yield incomplete mental files on animals.

Neuroscience research demonstrates that the more content we have, the more our brain develops to support that content. Every time we learn something, we build new neuronal connections or we solidify the connections we already have. But if we don't exercise our brains, those connections weaken and eventually die. This is where the oft-heard phrase "use it or lose it" originates.

So in many ways it is clear that bullet point five listed earlier may be the most accurate description of the relationship between development and learning. A brain's developmental stage determines what and when we can learn, which in turn facilitates the growth of more developmental capabilities. The period when each factor matters more in this cycle is age-dependent. In particular, periods when *synaptogenesis* occurs are called *sensitive periods*, which is when the brain is most malleable and most open to change.

For example, during synaptogenesis in late infancy, children are able to acquire different languages at an alarming rate. Because the neuronal pathways are resetting, they can be (re)shaped. If children are exposed to multiple languages consistently early in their life, they have a much higher chance of learning those languages than if they attempt to learn them later in life when the brain is much more developed. A natural developmental process is more important to educational outcomes than content at this point in development.

Conversely, if we continue the example of language, high school students taking French for the first time will learn it much faster if they've already learned Spanish. The similarities in the phonemic and grammatical structures facilitate the acquisition of a new language. In this instance, it is not a developmental process that enhances educational outcomes; it is the presence of preexisting content knowledge.

The older the children get, the slower they develop and the more content and skills they possess. Concurrent slow development and increased learning suggest that development is most important to education early in life, whereas prior learning is most important by adolescence. There are of course exceptions to the rule, but in general, when thinking about your child's schooling experiences, their developmental capacities should dictate educational decision-making.

TAKEAWAYS

Developmental psychology is all about the natural progression of children's physical, cognitive, and social/emotional capacities. Just like in schools, developmental psychologists work with children in specific age-groups. At each developmental stage, there are certain milestones we expect children to obtain. If they do not obtain them, it's not necessarily a cause for concern, but it may be a moment to pause and reflect on the factors influencing a child's development.

Barring any deviations from the normal developmental trajectory, when a child struggles in school, we turn to educational psychologists to offer support. Educational psychology bridges the gap between development and learning by studying factors influencing students' learning behaviors and outcomes. Neuroscience research provides a lot of information about how the brain functions and contributes to the development of brain-based instruction.

A normal developmental trajectory is cumulative and is heavily influenced by both genetics and environment. While all children are different, most children will be able to do similar things around the same time. Things like speaking are expected developmental milestones, but other abilities, like the ability to categorize objects by colors, are dependent upon a child's experience with different colored objects.

Whether or not development precedes learning or learning leads to development depends on the age of the child. Developmental capacities are really important from birth through early childhood; but by middle childhood, what a child already knows and can do serves as a catalyst for more cognitive development.

The intersection of development and learning is complex mostly because children are always developing. Whether it's physical growth, the ability to take others' perspective, or a shift in a friend group, the way children change affects how they engage in their own learning. When you understand where your child is on the developmental continuum, you can make informed decisions about what they will need at school to get them to that next developmental milestone.

Vocabulary to Know

Associated Words/Phrases	Definition
Processing speed	The fluency with which the brain performs routine tasks
Goal-directed behavior	Behaviors with specific intentions
Attachment	The emotional bond between a child and caregiver
Temperament	A person's emotional reactions to stimuli
Frontal lobe	Area of the brain responsible for executive functions (judgment, decision-making, planning)
Information processing	What the brain does with information
Egocentrism	Seeing the world only from one's own perspective
Social self	A flexible social identity usually seen in adolescents
Crowd	A large interest-based social group
Ideal self	The person adolescents hope to become
Learning style	The ways in which people process information best (includes visual, auditory, kinesthetic/tactile)
Learning disability	Difficulty acquiring or processing information and skills at age-expectant levels
Operant conditioning	Using rewards and punishments to change behavior
Classical conditioning	Associating specific stimuli with desired responses. Ex: when a teacher raises her hand, students stop speaking
Self-regulatory learning strategies	Behaviors such as organization, goal-setting, and environmental structuring that students' use to achieve academic success
Receptive skills	Cognitive processes involved in the input of new information
Procedural skills	Cognitive processes involved in the interpretation and manipulation of information
Expressive skills	Cognitive processes involved in the output of information
Temporal lobe	Area of the brain responsible for auditory processing
Parietal lobe	Area of the brain responsible for sensory information such as taste and touch
Cerebellum	Area of the brain responsible for balance and muscle coordination
Occipital lobe	Area of the brain responsible for visual processing
Synaptic pruning	Removing extraneous neural connections to improve efficiency
Hippocampus	Area of the brain responsible for long-term memory and emotions
Zone of proximal development	The distance between what a child can do on their own and what they can do with assistance
Schemata	Mental files about different topics
Assimilation	Incorporating new information into existing mental files
Accommodation	Altering or creating new mental files to incorporate new information
Overextension	A child's use of a single word to apply to many similar concepts
Synaptogenesis	A process through which unused neural connections are shed and reorganized
Sensitive periods	A point in development when a person is more receptive to specific stimuli, and when frequently used connections are strengthened

Figure 2.1

Chapter Three

Temperament, Personality, and How They Affect Learning

My children are so different from one another but I never thought about what that means in terms of their schooling.

—Mother of two college students

TEMPERAMENT

Shortly after birth it's clear what someone's temperament is. It's common to hear parents refer to their baby as fussy or happy or easygoing. At such a young age, those words are used to describe a baby's natural reaction to stimuli. Some babies cry when startled, while others appear confused. Some babies love to be swaddled and held closely against dad's chest, while others prefer space to move freely.

What's interesting is that these emotional and behavioral reactions to stimuli remain stable throughout life. Babies who rarely cry will grow into toddlers who rarely cry. By the time they are adolescents, what used to be a blessing turns into concern for a teenager who doesn't show emotion easily. Unlike physical and cognitive attributes, temperament remains pretty consistent, causing developmental psychologists to determine that temperament is a genetic trait.

Because temperament is something you're born with, most of the research conducted about temperament is done with infants. Psychologists measure temperament by considering the variety of ways a baby interacts with their environment. Included in those measurements are:

• *Activity level*—the level of movement and the amount of time spent moving.

- *Rhythmicity*—how you physiologically create (or don't create) bodily routines for sleeping, eating, and going to the bathroom.
- *Approach-withdrawal*—your initial response to something new.
- *Adaptability*—how quickly you adjust to new situations.
- *Threshold of responsiveness*—the intensity level required to evoke an emotional or behavioral response.
- *Intensity of reaction*—the energy level of a response.
- *Quality of mood*—the amount of positive versus negative behaviors within a limited period of time.
- *Distractibility*—the extent to which new stimuli disrupt or change ongoing behaviors.
- *Attention span*—the extent to which an activity is maintained.

All of these indicators help answer the question, "*how* is my child?" The answer may not be consistent across all nine measurements, but the combined answers help psychologists determine a child's temperament.

Early research by Chess and Thomas (1996) led to three widely used classifications: easy babies, difficult babies, and slow-to-warm-up babies. Easy babies are playful, routine, and adaptive to new situations. Difficult babies can be irritable, don't have consistent bodily routines, and react negatively to new situations. Slow-to-warm-up babies take a little time to adjust to stimuli and tend to be low in activity level.

Other research (Rothbart, Ahadi, and Evans, 2000) classifies babies according to their reactivity, affect, and self-regulation. For the most part, these measures are similar to the above-listed bullet points. All nine indicators represent a child's general disposition that describes how they interact with their environment.

Temperament at school. Just as a person's temperament is stable across time, it is also stable across settings. How a child reacts to stimuli at home is the same way they will react at school. Parents often neglect to consider their child's emotional needs when choosing schools because how schools accommodate students' emotions is difficult to ascertain.

On a school-wide level, behavior policies are one way in which schools reveal their approach to children's emotional needs. Schools with strict rules such as walking silently through the halls in a straight line, waiting to be called on to speak, or stringent dress codes are sending the message that children need to adapt to their environment, not the other way around.

Children who adjust easily to new situations will probably be fine in such a school. They will learn the rules, follow them, and likely never speak about them. But children who need consistency across home and school will have a harder time navigating the differences between the two settings. This may emerge in what schools call "disruptive behavior." Rarely are children purposefully being disruptive; often it's the result of a mismatch between home and school rules.

While many traditional public and private schools have strict behavior expectations, Montessori and Waldorf schools do not. Because of their pedagogical approaches (described in Chapter 1), children who attend these schools are given more freedom to learn in ways natural to them. There are few time restrictions, no standardized method of teaching, and less stringent rules. Teachers construct learning environments catered to children's emotional needs.

We see this intentionality in teachers' development of a *classroom climate*. Some children need more emotional support than others. A strong student–teacher relationship can go a long way in helping children feel appreciated and included in their classroom. Calling students by name, allowing them some agency in their learning, and valuing their individual contributions to the classroom are great ways that teachers help students be comfortable at school.

A teacher who also fosters positive peer relationships through collaborative work can be good for children who are a bit timid or slow to warm up. Conversely, this type of classroom can be overwhelming for kids who enjoy working alone and react negatively to too much noise and movement. The best classrooms offer both cooperative and individualized learning so all children are emotionally comfortable while also being pushed to learn in new ways.

Similarly, the pedagogy, or teaching practices, need to challenge children to become *self-regulated learners* while also honoring the unique learning needs of each child. When it comes to temperament, the most important pedagogical practice is teacher feedback. How a teacher critiques or praises a student can elicit very different emotions in different children.

For example, a child who is sensitive (i.e., reacts strongly to stimuli) may interpret a teacher's negative feedback as hurtful or mean. This could be a low score on a paper or an admonishment about misbehavior. Often, young children who are sensitive will believe their teacher doesn't like them, and, in turn, emotionally disconnect from the teacher and their learning experience.

Another child could be given the same negative feedback from the same teacher in the same classroom and interpret it entirely differently. A child who is "easygoing" is unlikely to be overly affected by the feedback and may not attend to it at all (which is another problem!). While it is indeed a teacher's job to determine which students need what kinds of feedback, parents should communicate their child's emotional needs to the teacher.

Emotional needs should also include the time needed for emotional and cognitive adjustment. In our current era of accountability, teachers are responsible for a lot of content in a short period of time. This means the pacing of class, especially in middle and high school, can be very fast. Kids who take a long time to transition between activities will struggle in a fast paced classroom where they are asked to start and stop activities often. It makes sense then that their emotional reaction is frustration.

Children who are asked to learn in contexts uncomfortable to them are being asked to complete an almost impossible task. Given that temperament does not change, it is unreasonable to ask a child to change how they feel while at school. It makes more sense to focus on changing the school, or to focus on the aspects of your child that are open to influence.

PERSONALITY

If temperament answers *how* a child is, personality is all about *who* a child is. A person's personality is best thought of as their patterns of feeling, thinking, and behaving in various circumstances. Personality emerges as temperament integrates with cognitive abilities, emotional regulation, and experiences. In other words, who someone is is a result of how they interact with their environment and their ability to shape those interactions.

The shaping of social environments is a *nurture component* of development (temperament is a *nature component*). With whom a child lives, the types of food they eat, the activities in which they engage, and even the language they speak affect who a child becomes. While environmental structuring is done by parents and family members, how a child participates in their environment is largely influenced by their temperament.

In a household with a lot of children, a sensitive child may prefer to spend time alone in their room. Their chosen separation from the larger social environment means they may miss certain experiences, such as being taught to cook, but spend more time engaging in other activities like reading. Over time, they may develop a deep interest in literature and have no desire to cook. This aspect of their personality—that they like to read—is a result of the interaction between their temperament and their environment.

Although we label personalities the same way we label temperaments, the nuances of personality are much more complex. Who someone is is not only a result of their temperament and the environments to which they've been exposed, but also of the decisions they make about how they shape their environment.

Children who prefer solitude and read a lot will likely choose extracurricular activities that indulge their interest in reading and need for solitude (like a book club). Through that activity they meet other people who share this interest, and are simultaneously able to enhance their skill level in their chosen activity. They may then major in English or Comparative Literature in college, and choose to become a novelist.

This simplistic timeline is a good example of how personality functions as a feedback loop. Initial behaviors borne of the temperament-environment interaction become preferences we indulge by shaping our environment to support those behaviors. This is how someone comes to be known as a "quiet person" or "deep thinker"—descriptions we use to label personality types.

Because there is a feedback loop wherein we reinforce our own natural interests, we restrict our exposure to other activities which could bring enjoyment. Further, we shape our environments so we interact with the same kind of people repeatedly.

For psychologists, this is concerning because young children and adolescents need diverse environments to foster diverse social and cognitive skills during heightened periods of developmental plasticity. School offers a setting in which children can be pushed to encounter people and experiences that contribute to personality formation.

Personality at school. "My child would never do that!" So often parents are surprised by the reports they get from teachers about how their child behaves at school. In reality, it shouldn't be surprising that children behave differently in different environments. Even children as young as 10 months are savvy enough to know when and with whom they can behave in certain ways. Though behaviorally concerning, this type of manipulation is indicative of advanced cognition.

For a child to associate specific rules, behaviors, and emotions with specific people requires a high level of reflection and *abstract thought*. Some children do this subconsciously but most do it purposefully to shape their environments to suit their personal desires. It is natural to try to change an environment to fit you, but when it comes to school, this is rarely effective. Instead, confused parents can't figure out why their child is such a different person at school.

To solve the mystery, parents need to only pause and think about their child's temperament, talents/skills, and interests. Then think about the context of school where, by early adolescence, children spend the majority of their time. If there is not a good fit between what children want to do and what they are allowed to do, it makes sense that children will try to force that fit.

Before enrolling a child in school, parents should carefully consider who their child is and what kind of environment facilitates success for their child. Equally as important is deciding who you'd like your child to become. Given the amount of time spent with peers, friends have a larger influence on the cultivation of certain behaviors than parents. And while parents can't always control with whom their child spends time, they can control the context in which social interactions occur.

More specifically, school is the perfect place to help shape a child's personality. Though seemingly cunning at first, this parenting decision is no different than assigning chores, giving a curfew, or limiting the amount of candy kids eat. Whether children are at home or school, parents have specific values and beliefs they wish to impart to their children. They do this by structuring children's lives in ways that reinforce those values.

A similar structuring technique can be applied to choosing schools and teachers. Like when considering temperamental fit, the classroom climate can be highly influential on children's developing personalities. Every classroom has behavioral expectations that set the stage for social skill development. Especially in elementary and middle schools, children learn about intergroup relations, how to read social cues, use body language, and when and how to speak formally with teachers versus casually with friends.

The amount of social interaction in a classroom can be the difference between a "social butterfly" who's been practicing social skills since pre-school, and an introvert who is not temperamentally shy but may not have had the opportunity to engage in meaningful social interactions. Like any skill, social interactions take practice, and school is where children develop their social selves.

The curriculum is another key player in classroom dynamics. The curriculum is *what* is taught (as opposed to *how* it is taught), and is therefore students' entry into new content and new experiences. If there are music, art, or technology classes, kids may discover an interest or talent hitherto unknown. Physical education (PE) class is a good place to refine motor skills, balance, and coordination. PE is where some children realize they are actually kinesthetic learners.

Similarly, the extracurricular offerings in schools are often critical to an educational experience. Whether it's chess club or cheerleading, after-school activities offer children a place to indulge their interests while perhaps encouraging the development of new interests. It is not uncommon for middle and high schoolers to join a club just because their best friend is doing it. Without those opportunities children may never channel their nonstop chatter into debating.

As important as the curriculum is, the delivery of the curriculum matters too. Teaching methods like lecturing do not work for everyone. Discussion-based classes, hands-on experiences, and using technology are alternative ways for students to engage with course content. They may discover that, when given the opportunity, they prefer using a computer to doing an experiment.

Each of these factors (classroom climate, curriculum, extracurriculars, and pedagogy) has the possibility of exposing children to new people, content, and behaviors—the very things that shape personalities. Having conversations about their school experience is a good way to involve children in their own learning. This prompts them to reflect on which aspects of schooling are and are not aligned with who they are and what they need for academic achievement.

Like everything in parenting, there is a balance between pushing kids beyond their comfort zone and ensuring they are in an academic setting conducive to their success. It may take a couple of tries, but careful observation and conversation can facilitate a schooling experience that helps your children grow into the person they want to be and you want them to become.

TAKEAWAYS

Most people consider temperament and personality to be the same thing. This is logical because one's personality is a direct reflection of one's temperament; however, they develop differently and have different implications for children's schooling. While temperament is largely a result of genetics, personality is more a result of the interactions between genetics and social environments.

This means that while it's possible to help shape children's interests and talents, it is not possible to change how they interact with the world. Given the stability of temperament, parents and families should consider children's emotional needs before their social needs when choosing schools. Most critical to emotional well-being are strong student-teacher relationships through which teachers are responsive to students' varying needs for support and inclusion.

Most important to personality development are the curricula both in and out of the classroom. What children learn in school can often define the breadth of their knowledge and the depth of their interest in diverse topics. Further, extracurricular activities can be the sole place children interact with people and ideas beyond the scope of classroom learning.

But as children progress through school, teachers change, the curriculum changes, and children change. Cognitive, emotional, and social advancements alter the way kids interact with the world; thus, their personality is likely to adjust accordingly. Some interests will come and go while others form the core of their social activities. A BFF (best friend forever) in middle school may be only an acquaintance in high school. Just as parents accept these natural developmental progressions, they must also be on the lookout for accompanying changes in the student-school fit.

Temperament and personality are equally as important in development and should therefore be considered equally but separately in educational decision-making. A good fit between a school's culture and a child's emotional and social needs can be the difference between academic success and academic disengagement. Meetings with teachers, classroom observations, and conversations with other parents can provide insight into what schools and teachers value in students' learning.

REFERENCES

Chess, S., and Thomas, A. (1996). *Temperament: Theory and practice*. New York: Brunner-Mazel.

Rothbart, M. K., Ahadi, S. A., and Evans, D. E. (2000). Temperament and personality: Origins and outcomes. *Journal of Personality and Social Psychology*, 78(1), 122–135.

Vocabulary to Know	
Associated Words/Phrases	Definition
Classroom climate	The social and emotional "feel" of a classroom
Pedagogy	How a teacher teaches; the instructional methods used
Self-regulated learning	Learning in which a student develops and refines learning strategies based upon feedback from teachers and their own self-evaluation
Pacing	The speed at which a teacher moves through the curriculum
Emotional regulation	A conscious process through which one modifies one's emotional state
Nurture component of development	Environmental contributions to development
Nature component of development	Genetic contributions to development
Plasticity	The degree to which natural development is open to influence
Abstract thought	Higher order thinking that involves reasoning, logic, and/or sequencing
Social self	A flexible social identity usually seen in adolescents
Kinesthetic learning	Also called tactile learning; Learning involving physical movement
School culture	The norms and values that guide school functioning; Often reflected in academic and behavioral policies

Figure 3.1

Chapter Four

The Nature(?) of Intelligence

Isn't the whole point of school to make my kid smarter?
—Father of a 5th grader

INTELLIGENCE

What we know about intelligence is actually not a lot. Despite studying it for 100 years, psychologists have no single definition of what it means to be intelligent. We've moved through at least four widely accepted definitions, but even some of those are more like descriptors than definitions. What psychologists have agreed upon is that intelligence is not about what you know; it's about what you can do with the knowledge you have.

In 1904, British psychologist Charles Spearman published work discussing intelligence as having two factors: general and specific. The *general factor* is comprised of cognitive skills that can be applied across domains and activities. The *specific factor* refers to a collection of cognitive skills that only apply to activities within a single domain. The most important thing about Spearman's theory is that he believed people could be either generally or specifically intelligent. This was the first time we thought of intelligence as categorical.

While we still believe that intelligence is domain-specific, David Wechsler's *global capacity view* of intelligence suggests that intelligence is more than what can be measured on tests. He cites creativity, goal-setting, and the development of morals as equally important as cognitive skills like processing speed and memory retrieval. He proposed that intelligent people act purposefully, think rationally, and can move through diverse environments effortlessly.

47

So far, both conceptualizations of intelligence are a bit vague and hard to measure. To better capture more specific components of intelligence, Robert Sternberg proposed his *triarchic theory of intelligence* in 2002. This theory states that intelligence has three main parts: practical ability (adapting to and shaping one's environment), creative ability (solving unfamiliar problems), and analytical ability (using prior knowledge and skills to learn new information).

Howard Gardener expanded on this theory and offered the world of educational psychology his theory of *multiple intelligences*, which tells us the specific domains in which people apply their practical, creative, and analytical abilities. Easily the most popular theory of intelligence in the realm of education, Gardener outlines eight forms of intelligence:

1. Logical-mathematical (numbers, reason, logic)
2. Linguistic (sounds, meanings, and functions of words)
3. Musical (rhythm, pitch, and timbre)
4. Spatial (visualization, mechanics)
5. Bodily kinesthetic (body control)
6. Interpersonal (attuned to the moods of other people)
7. Intrapersonal (attuned to one's own internal mental and emotional processing)
8. Naturalist (attuned to the environment; care for living beings)

Teachers especially love this theory because it allows them to find brilliance in every student. But Gardner warns us that just because two children have strong logical-mathematical intelligence does not mean their strengths will emerge in the same way. One child might love math class and do extremely well on anything to do with numbers. The other child might prefer to spend her time creating her own math problems rather than solving them.

Similarly, just because a child demonstrates overall competency in a specific domain does not mean they will be great at every task under that umbrella. A child with great linguistic intelligence may read three grade levels ahead but have a hard time writing an essay. Gardner's theory is simply underscoring Spearman's point that intelligence is not an all-or-nothing phenomenon.

In fact, it is widely believed by psychologists that intelligence functions on a continuum and is heavily influenced by a child's developmental stage. Decades of research have found that cognitive and behavioral skills can emerge and disappear depending upon how often someone uses them. These findings have forced psychologists to develop definitions of intelligence that acknowledge its evolving nature.

Psychology professor Raymond Nickerson of Tufts University offers a broad definition that seems to capture what most people mean when they call someone intelligent:

> [They have] the ability to learn, to reason well, to solve novel problems, and to deal effectively with the challenges—often unpredictable—that confront one in daily life. (Nickerson, 2011, p. 108)

As you can see, this definition is an attempt to combine many theories of intelligence. It is not the go-to definition by any means, but it offers us a place to start when we think about assessing just how smart someone really is.

IQ TESTING

To quantify someone's intelligence is a difficult task, but we attempt to do so through intelligence testing, often termed *IQ testing*. IQ stands for "intelligence quotient" and is calculated by dividing a mental age (as determined through testing) by a chronological age and multiplying by 100. In recent years, we've moved away from such a simplistic formula for IQ toward assessments that measure dozens of cognitive skills on a developmental trajectory.

The most common tests are the Stanford-Binet Intelligence Scales, the Wechsler Intelligence Scale for Children, and the Wechsler Adult Intelligence Scale (do any of these names look familiar?). Each test is comprised of subtests across multiple domains and skills such as word recognition, pattern identification, mental arithmetic, and memory.

A person's performance on a particular subtest is compared to the average performance of people in that person's age group. The results help identify if, and where, a person is performing above or below what is expected in normal development. Though it is possible to calculate a global IQ score by averaging scores across all subtests, it is more common for educational psychologists to calculate an IQ score for each subtest because that information is helpful in identifying a child's areas of strength and areas in need of improvement.

There are, of course, limitations to what IQ tests can tell us. First, the name "IQ" is misleading. Many psychologists prefer to call these tests "scholastic aptitude tests" or "tests of school ability." Because we aren't really sure what intelligence is, we measure the skills we know make one successful in school and in life. We may be missing dozens of cognitive skills simply because we haven't yet identified them as conducive to academic achievement.

Second, IQ tests are merely our best approximation of what is happening in the brain. We can only measure the outcomes of brain processes (e.g., what someone says or does), not the processes themselves. Our results are therefore only as good as our tests.

If the questions about pattern identification are too easy, we will end up with an overestimation of someone's visual processing skills. If the word recognition questions include words unfamiliar to nonnative English speakers, the results will underestimate language skills. If the test has not been norm-referenced with an appropriate age group, the scoring will not be applicable to all students.

This is why it's extremely important that parents and teachers consult an educational psychologist when they want to measure children's intelligence. Educational psychologists will use the best tests to measure the skills you want measured. They are also trained to properly interpret test results, and to make accompanying educational recommendations.

Last, and perhaps most important, is that IQ tests are only a snapshot in time. Many parents and teachers mistakenly interpret IQ scores as finite. Because the tests measure skills that can be enhanced with practice, it is very likely that people can improve their performance on IQ tests. In fact, research demonstrates that a person's IQ score can vary 15 to 30 points from one testing to another.

This may not sound like a lot, but given that IQ is measured in 15-point increments, an increase of 30 points is significant. If you first scored a 115 and later a 145, the second test would move you from an above average performance to genius-level! An IQ score is just a reflection of how a child performed on a particular test on a particular day compared to children of the same age.

NEUROMYTHS

Our misunderstanding of intelligence and our misuse of IQ tests have led to some widely accepted misconceptions about whether, and how, people become smarter.

Learning styles. Not a single conversation about teaching or learning can happen without the common phrase *learning style*. What exactly is a learning style? Most people give an answer that in some way references the way your brain thinks or processes information. To an extent, that is true. But learning styles are preferences borne of experience, not predetermined ways of thinking based upon mysterious brain wiring.

Learning styles are adaptive and situational. The way you take notes, study, or even engage in conversation is dependent upon the subject matter, the people in the room, and social expectations. For example, to solve even simple math problems, many people have to write them down or use their fingers to count. Common lingo would call this *kinesthetic learning*.

But most people don't draw sketches of paintings in order to understand them; you simply stare at the image and perhaps tilt your head one way or another. This is *visual learning*. Neither is better or worse than the other, but one is more efficient at processing symbolic representations than the other. Your brain will always default to the most efficient mode of processing to save cognitive resources.

For most people, the most efficient mode is the mode with the strongest and most plentiful neural pathways. Depending upon children's prior learning experiences in and out of school, they will be more efficient at processing information in particular ways.

For example, if your child has been in Montessori school for most of their schooling, they probably will consider themselves as a kinesthetic learner. This is because Montessori pedagogy is hands-on and center-based. Students learn by doing. Since almost all of their learning has occurred in this fashion, the neural pathways in the parietal lobe (our sensory lobe) are likely more refined than in the occipital lobe (visual) and temporal lobe (auditory).

But that doesn't mean pathways in the occipital and temporal lobes can't be used. With intentional practice, the brain can be trained. So while it is important to recognize and honor your child's learning preferences, it is also necessary that they are challenged to think about information in multiple ways.

The gendered brain. People often say girls are left-brained and boys are right-brained. This is because girls are thought to be better at speaking, reading, and writing, and it just so happens that the left hemisphere of the brain is responsible for language processing. Boys, on the other hand, are said to be good with numbers, mechanics, and other visuospatial processing—all tasks housed in the right hemisphere (along with facial recognition and musicality).

This myth is a bit of a chicken or an egg issue. It seems as though the myth originated by observing the skills in which each gender exceled. Based upon those results, once we knew where those skills were located in the brain, a myth was born. But, in fact, neuroscience research suggests we should think about academic skills from the inside-out. Girls and boys may excel at different tasks because their brains are developing differently.

These differences are likely caused by a mix of nature (genetics) and nurture (environment). Why girls' brains develop faster than boys' brains is not fully understood, but as mentioned in Chapter 2, research hints that hormone production has something to do with it. This faster development means that girls are able to engage in complex cognitive tasks a bit earlier than boys, and language is considered the brain's most difficult task.

If we also consider the influence of the environment, cultural gender norms play a huge role in how we train the brain to think. Both parents and teachers interact with boys and girls differently, often with different behavioral expectations. Even from birth, the way parents speak to boys and girls hints at the implicit expectations we have for our children's language skills.

Infant girls hear more words than infant boys and are more likely to engage in back-and-forth vocalization. Both boys and girls experience language more from women (mom) than men (dad), thus introducing the association between language and femininity early in life. We further reinforce this association through the conversations we have with children, the chores we require them to do, the toys we buy them, and even the way they are treated in school.

Girls are called on more than boys, are more likely to be disciplined for disruptive talking, and are graded harsher than boys on literacy tasks. Even in college, girls are encouraged to major in word-heavy disciplines like English and History whereas boys are advised to major in science or math. Such gendered expectations inevitably mean girls rehearse their language skills more than boys, so of course their brains are better word processors.

The brain can do anything! In the early 2000s something interesting emerged to unite parenting, neuroscience, and learning: Baby Einstein products. Baby Einstein is a line of products produced by Disney and advertised to make your child smarter—even sometimes in utero. These products include mobiles, books, videos, games, and more. Once these "educational toys" hit the market, pregnant moms with headphones draped across their bellies were a common sight.

Commercials with happy and excited kids engaging in reading, writing, and math made parents rush to stores to buy products that would ensure admission to Harvard. Since 1998, consumers have spent, on average, 1 billion dollars annually to ensure their kids had every cognitive advantage. For almost a decade, parents lived blissfully thinking they were giving their kid a leg up in the educational market by purchasing Baby Einstein products.

But in 2007 research emerged to suggest that for every hour spent watching Baby Einstein DVDs, babies knew seven or eight fewer words than a baby who didn't watch those videos. After a contentious legal battle, other scholars changed the results saying that while the DVDs produced no reliable cognitive advantage for babies, they also don't cause harm.

Millions of parents were stunned to learn that the hundreds of dollars they spent on educational toys would've been better spent on children's books. Many parents thought the Baby Einstein products were an updated version of the 1990s sensation Hooked on Phonics (which did prove to be effective at increasing children's reading fluency).

Hooked on Phonics was effective because it capitalized on an age-old learning principle: rehearsal. Children viewed flashcards and books with different phonemic combinations until they could identify sound codes and letters with lightning speed. This content knowledge helped kids read faster and more accurately. Simple.

But Baby Einstein DVDs were operating on a flawed assumption—that children can learn just as well from video (and other types of technology) as they can from a human. In fact, research suggests that children always learn better with a human teacher because humans provide contextual clues through body language and facial expressions that help children interpret new information.

Further, kids also need an opportunity to actively participate in the learning process instead of passively listening or watching (this is why Dora the Explorer pauses for kids to answer questions). Without guided instruction and some type of feedback, Baby Einstein products initially missed the cognitive mark (more recent products are better aligned with neuroscience research).

It's not surprising that parents were quick to believe in the wonder of these products. All parents want the best for their children and if a fun game can give them a leg up, why not? The marketing was genius because it capitalized on the commonly held belief that the brain can learn passively. In fact, many people believe the brain is so awesome, you can learn while you sleep.

While the brain is indeed an amazing organ, receiving, interpreting, and storing information requires some intentionality and, well, consciousness. The brain *is* extremely active while you sleep, but it is organizing the information you already have, not acquiring more. A sleeping brain is refining neural pathways and ensuring the brain is working properly. So yes, sleep supports optimal learning, but it is not the process through which you learn.

MINDSETS

If you really want to know how to make your kids smarter, you need to look at their beliefs about their own intelligence. Research demonstrates that what matters for intellectual growth is what one believes about one's own capacity to learn. Dr. Carol Dweck and her colleague, Dr. Lisa Blackwell, conducted research on how children's beliefs about effort influence their academic achievement.

What they've found is that children (and adults) generally have one of two mindsets about intelligence: a *fixed* mindset or a *growth* mindset. People who believe that intelligence is predetermined and that no amount of effort will change their achievement have a fixed mindset. Children with fixed mindsets will often say things like, "I'm just not a math person" or "there's no point in trying."

When faced with a choice between a difficult and an easy task, a child with a fixed mindset will choose the easier task to ensure success. In other words, people with fixed mindsets have a hard time managing failure. They see failure as a reflection of their intelligence instead of an opportunity for improvement.

If a child has a growth mindset, on the other hand, they view failure as a reflection of their effort and not their ability. They will often say, "I could've done better if I studied more" or "if I try hard enough, I can be smarter." These children will almost always choose the harder task in an attempt to challenge themselves. If they don't succeed fully, children with a growth mind-set are open to feedback.

The combination of a willingness to fail, openness to feedback, and belief in their capacity to learn make a growth mindset more conducive to academic achievement than a fixed mindset. In fact, one study found that 7th grade students with growth mindsets had increased math achievement over two years compared to students with a fixed mindset. It was so much better that growth mindsets predicted math scores 1 standard deviation above the mean and fixed mindsets predicted math scores 1 standard deviation below the mean.

Because mindsets matter so much, it's extremely important to foster a growth mindset where children view themselves as active agents in their learning. When adults praise high grades, being on the honor roll, or receiving a trophy, they are telling a child that what matters in the learning process is the outcome. And because an outcome cannot be changed, children interpret their performance as unchangeable.

Conversely, when adults praise children's learning processes, they are telling children that their effort is what's most important to their learning. While an A on a spelling test should be celebrated, it is important that adults model appropriate *causal attribution* processes and help children think through why they earned an A. So instead of saying "You're so smart!" try saying, "Wow! You must've studied hard for the test!" Then sit back and watch your child become a spelling genius!

TAKEAWAYS

It should be clear now that intelligence is not what you know; it's what you have the capacity to learn. The ways we measure intelligence depend on a lot: the tests we use, the outcomes we care about, and the way we define intelligence. No matter which intelligence theory you endorse, what is most important is that you remember that a child's intelligence is not fixed. With effort, challenge-seeking, and healthy conversations, all children can learn.

Unfortunately we don't always give children opportunities to learn, because we have some misconceptions about what our brains can and can't do. Neuromyths related to learning styles, girl-vs-boy brains, and passive learning techniques engender inaccurate educational expectations. The truth is that our brains can learn any information presented in any format, but depending upon prior experience, some formats are more accessible than others.

Indeed, people do have stronger abilities in certain domains over others, but they also have the capacity to improve in weaker areas. The feedback children receive from parents and teachers directly relates to their beliefs about their own intelligence. Praising children for outcomes reinforces the idea that their intelligence can't be changed. When we praise children for their hard work, we teach them that effort—not innate ability—is what led to honor roll.

Intelligence is the accumulation of cognitive skills. Like all skills, cognitive skills can be improved upon with practice. People can become smarter if they consciously challenge themselves to do things that don't come easily to them. So even though your child is a genius, they too have room for improvement. With the proper encouragement and focus on areas of weakness, you will discover that the sky really is the limit when it comes to intelligence.

REFERENCES

American Academy of Pediatrics (2001). Children, adolescents, and television. *Pediatrics*, 107(2), 423–426.

Blackwell, L. A., Trzesniewski, K. H., and Dweck, C. S. (2007). Theories of intelligence and achievement across the junior high school transition: A longitudinal study and intervention. *Child Development*, 78, 246–263.

Dweck, C. S. (2006). *Mindset*. New York, NY: Random House.

Ferguson, C. J., and Donnellan, M. B. (2013). Is the association between children's baby video viewing and poor language development robust? A reanalysis of Zimmerman, Christakis, and Meltzoff (2007). *Developmental Psychology*, 50(1), 129–137.

Gardener, H. (2006). *Multiple intelligences: New horizons* (Rev. ed.). New York: Basic Books.

Nickerson, R. S. (2011). Developing intelligence through instruction. In R. S. Sternberg and S. B. Kaufman (Eds.), *The Cambridge handbook of intelligence* (pp. 107–129). New York: Cambridge University Press.

Sternberg, R. J. (2002). Intelligence is not just inside the head: The theory of successful intelligence. In J. Aronson (Ed.), *Improving academic achievement* (pp. 227–244). San Diego, CA: Academic Press.

Wechsler, D. (1975). Intelligence defined and undefined: A relativistic appraisal. *American Psychologist*, 30(2), 135–139.

Vocabulary to Know	
Associated Words/Phrases	Definition
General factor of intelligence	Cognitive skills that are used across domains
Domain	A topical area such as "math" or "language"
Specific factor of intelligence	Cognitive skills that are used within specific domains
Global capacity view of intelligence	Intelligence is more than what is measured on tests
Triarchic theory of intelligence	Intelligence comes in three forms: practical, creative, and analytical
Multiple intelligence theory	Intelligence comes in eight forms: logical-mathematical, linguistic, musical, spatial, bodily-kinesthetic, interpersonal, intrapersonal, and naturalist
IQ testing	Series of assessments done to measure specific cognitive abilities across many domains
Norm-referenced tests	Tests that report how results compare to an average hypothetical test taker who is demographically similar to the test taker
Learning style	The ways in which people process information best (includes visual, auditory, kinesthetic/tactile)
Kinesthetic Learning	Learning involving physical body movements. Also referred to as hands-on learning
Visual learning	Learning involving watching, observing, reading, or other engagement of the eyes
Fixed mindset	The belief that intelligence is predetermined and cannot be changed regardless of effort
Growth mindset	The belief that intelligence can be increased with appropriate effort and challenge

Figure 4.1

Chapter Five

Developmental Outliers

My kid isn't like other kids.

—Mother of an autistic student

GIFTEDNESS

Giftedness is an umbrella term encompassing a variety of learning differences. In school settings, giftedness is used to describe students who consistently outperform their peers on formative and summative assessments. Children can be broadly gifted, often indicating a high IQ, or they can be gifted in a particular area such as mathematics. Psychologists differentiate these types of giftedness as *domain general* and *domain specific*.

Some children are also gifted when it comes to particular cognitive skills such as visual processing, or they may have the ability to remember large amounts of information easily. The different classifications of giftedness do not make one child "more" gifted than another because giftedness, unlike IQ, does not operate on a continuum.

True giftedness is actually very rare. For psychologists, domain general giftedness is identified by an IQ score of at least 130, which is two standard deviations above the average IQ score of 100. It is believed that only 5% of the population has an IQ score above 125. So while almost every child is very good at something, very few children are very good at everything.

Research conducted by Robert Siegler, Professor of Psychology at Carnegie Mellon University, suggests that young children (up to age

11) experience a lot of *cognitive variability*—unstable differences in how they think. His work shows that children's thinking changes gradually over time. He called his theory "overlapping waves" because when mapped on a graph, children's use of mathematical strategies overlap with one another, flowing from one strategy to the next.

This suggests that on any given day, perhaps the day a student takes an IQ test, the student might be thinking in one way, but by following week, the student is thinking in a different way! Any IQ score garnered from a test the previous week may not represent a child's intellectual capabilities the following week. The constant evolution of children's cognition makes it very hard to determine giftedness.

Developmental and cognitive psychologists agree that around age 8, kids' brains start to settle into consistent patterns of thinking, so cognitive test scores begin to be a bit more reliable around 3rd grade. But because children's brains reboot during puberty (remember *synaptogenesis?*), it is recommended that children be retested every few years to maintain accurate identification of their learning needs.

But this rarely happens. Processes for identifying giftedness vary widely depending upon school district, school building, and classroom. Because of the financial and time commitment involved in cognitive testing, and the presence of at least a dozen different IQ tests, most schools rely on teachers to identify gifted students in their classrooms. You can imagine that this method is almost never accurate.

Most students identified as gifted are not actually gifted (sorry!). Classroom teachers are not trained psychologists, so they are poor evaluators of cognitive strengths and weaknesses. Teachers compare students to other students they've taught, as opposed to the tens of thousands of students nationwide who are used to norm-reference IQ tests. Teachers just haven't interacted with enough students to be able to say what is average, above average, or exceptional.

Indeed, it is hard for teachers to distinguish between natural intellectual abilities and environmental influence. For example, a 2nd grade student who reads at the 5th grade level is not necessarily gifted. This student may come from a home where family members read to the student daily. The student might also have gone to a preschool that emphasized literacy skills. Oftentimes, especially in primary schools, what appears to be giftedness is a result of nurture, not nature. Or in more common terms, it's a result of exposure and practice, not bionic brain powers.

The reverse can happen as well. Many students with intellectual gifts—especially in artistic domains—are overlooked because they are not given the opportunity to display their gifts. Students who are musically inclined would only be recognized as gifted in a music class. Given that many public schools have eliminated music programs, the likelihood of a student discovering hidden musical talent is small (another reason to pay attention to course offerings when choosing schools!).

The students who end up being identified as gifted are a mix of truly gifted learners and those who are probably just good students. They behave well, turn in their work, ask questions, and consistently perform at the top of the class. They may also be creative, humorous, or show a deep interest in a particular subject. Because teachers are comparing your child to the other students in their class, as your child switches classrooms, the likelihood of your child being identified as gifted changes.

If in fact your child starts at a new school and is invited to the gifted program, do not assume the program will be the same as it was at their old school. The structure and purpose of gifted programs vary widely, thus creating diversity in the quality of programs between schools.

With respect to structure, pullout programs are the most common model of gifted education in public schools. The title "pullout" comes from the fact that students are pulled out of class to take one or more of their core subjects with other gifted students. Alternatively, core subjects can be taught in the regular classroom and gifted periods can be used for creative projects. These creative classes tend to be focused less on direct instruction and more on self-guided learning.

There is heavy criticism surrounding the pullout model of gifted education. The one-size-fits-all structure overlooks the individual needs of students. Truly gifted students do not often experience the academic rigor necessary to keep them engaged in school, while misidentified students can sometimes find the quantity of work and the pace overly taxing.

The project-based pullout program is especially concerning because there is no clear curriculum that is tied to academic standards, and the work is meant to be fun, not rigorous. While there may be lesson plans, projects, and even field trips, most project-based gifted classes do nothing to meet the academic needs of gifted students. Many kids use this time to hang out with friends and basically have a free period.

Just because the school has recommended that your child enroll in the gifted program does not mean it is an appropriate academic option. Before happily signing a form confirming your child's genius, you should observe a gifted class, speak with the teachers in the program, and request the curriculum. If you find it's not a good fit, consider consulting an educational psychologist for assistance in recommendations for learning supports.

In the meantime it's a good idea to talk to your child's teachers about what they are doing in the regular classroom to support gifted students. Their answers should be more than "allowing them to work ahead." Instead, challenge can happen through additional work, increasing the rigor of existing work, or by using different curricula or learning materials that are still at grade level, but may be more interdisciplinary, requiring students to think more complexly.

GIFTED PROGRAM PROFILE

The Charlotte Mecklenburg School district in Charlotte, North Carolina offers one of the only K-12 gifted programs in the nation. Their program, Horizons, is for exceptionally gifted students who need more rigor than a traditional classroom can offer. In academic year 2014–2015, the program served a total of 75 students in a district with over 145,000 students, representing just .05% of the student population.

The admissions process is rigorous and extensive. First, students must apply to the program. If invited for an interview, they are given the *Kaufman Test of Educational Achievement* (KTEA) and required to complete a writing sample. They must score a 98% on both reading and math sections of the KTEA and be scored above grade level on their writing sample.

They then take the Stanford-Binet-V aptitude test and the Iowa Test of Basic Skills (ITBS) achievement test before submitting two additional writing samples and three math samples to ensure the student is at least two grade levels ahead. A list of 10–15 recently read books and a letter of recommendation from a prior teacher complete an applicant's portfolio.

The portfolio is then reviewed by a committee and evaluated on a scale of 1–4 across six areas. Minimum points on the rubric represent an IQ score of 132–134 and 95% achievement on the ITBS. Maximum scores represent an IQ of 145+ and 98–99% achievement on the ITBS. A total score of 18 out of 24 is required for applicants to move to the final stage of the admissions process where they undergo a performance assessment worth another 4 points. An applicant must have a total of 22 out of 28 points to be considered for admission into Horizons.

Rising kindergartners, despite not having any formal schooling experience, must also participate in the full admissions process. Because they may not have teacher recommendations or past report cards to indicate their potential for achievement, Horizons requires that 4–5-year-old children must indicate competency in the following areas on their application:

- Read chapter books and comprehend them independently
- Write full stories with a clear beginning, middle, and end
- Subtract and add multidigit numbers
- Basic multiplication and division

For admitted students, transportation to and from their grade level school is provided at no expense to the parents. The students will then be placed in a classroom with their age peers instead of their intellectual peers. In elementary and middle schools, Horizons students are in self-contained classes where they take core subjects with a single teacher. They take electives and have lunch with same-age peers who are not Horizons students.

If a student is not admitted into the program, they can reapply after a 24-month waiting period, up to 8th grade. The high expectations of the Horizons program means that most students (85–90%) who apply are not accepted. In those events, it does not mean there is an absence of giftedness. It may suggest that this particular program is not a good fit for that particular child.

LEARNING DISABILITIES/DISORDERS

It is not uncommon for children with domain-specific giftedness to struggle in other areas. The brain, though divided into task-oriented lobes, is a self-balancing organ. When one area of the brain needs more resources, another area of the brain must sacrifice resources. This is the logic that explains why geniuses like Wolfgang Mozart and Leonardo Da Vinci are thought to have been mentally ill according to today's classification standards.

Though Mozart and Da Vinci are extreme examples, thousands of children experience academic struggles because their brains are similarly trying to allocate cognitive resources in an efficient manner. When it can't, there are deficits in particular cognitive skills that can make learning very difficult. When environmental factors are accounted for, many teachers and psychologists turn to organic—or brain-based—explanations for academic underperformance.

Learning disabilities and learning disorders occur in about 5% of public school students. Though these two terms are often used interchangeably, they represent different degrees of severity of learning difficulties. Learning disabilities occur when students are struggling with particular tasks in schools, but not enough to affect their overall schooling experience. A learning disability is usually domain specific.

Learning disorders are severe deficits that affect almost all aspects of a child's learning. The specific type of deficit tends to be domain general and may emerge in different ways in different tasks. Most students are diagnosed with learning disabilities and not disorders, but both involve problems with information processing either at the encoding, storage, or retrieval stages.

The most common learning disabilities in K-12 schools do indeed involve some kind of processing problem. Struggles with visual and auditory processing, dyslexia, dysgraphia, dyspraxia, dyscalculia, and dysphasia/aphasia, comprise the majority of learning diagnoses in schools. Health disabilities, emotional disturbances, physical disabilities, developmental delays, and autism are also included in national data on learning disabilities.

The presence of emotional disabilities can affect the emergence and treatment of cognitive disabilities. Especially important are emotional disorders including anxiety, attention deficit disorder (ADD), and attention deficit hyperactive disorder (ADHD). These diagnoses are increasingly common in schools and have prompted psychologists to study possible relationships between school factors (testing, class size, etc.) and student stress.

The processes for identifying and accommodating cognitive disabilities are more complicated than those for the more obvious emotional disabilities. Cognitive disabilities are first noticed by teachers and parents. Students may spend an abnormally long amount of time on a single task and still not perform well. They are often frustrated and can eventually disengage completely from learning because it is "too hard."

It can appear as though children are just not "trying hard enough" or "concentrating" on their work, when in fact they are using twice as much brain energy to complete a task as someone else. After a prolonged period of time, many students with undiagnosed learning difficulties avoid academic work all together.

Other students develop coping mechanisms to help them get through their work faster and more effectively. Sometimes these methods are ingenious and other times they are less than desirable. For example, students with processing struggles might record class sessions so they can replay them later when they have more time to think about what was said. Other students might think copying their notes multiple times will help them learn content.

When teachers notice a student is struggling, they will initiate a response to intervention (RTI). RTI is a multitiered process to help identify and respond to students' learning needs before classifying them as needing special education (and often as an intermediary step while waiting for cognitive testing to occur). RTIs involve a three-tier process: high quality instruction and group intervention, targeted intervention, and intensive intervention.

Students remain on level 1 for up to eight weeks as teachers deliver supplemental instruction and consistent evaluations to monitor students' progress. If students do not make adequate progress, they move to level 2 where they receive more frequent and intensive academic support in smaller groups. If after eight more weeks students are still struggling, they move to level 3 where they receive individualized support targeted at their specific deficits.

If a student is still having a difficult time after moving through the RTI process, a formal cognitive evaluation will be conducted by the school and the student may be eligible for special education services. Many parents choose to request the formal evaluation before their child moves through level 3 because, in general, the RTI process can last anywhere from a semester to an entire academic year.

Having children tested sooner can be a good idea because, when diagnosed appropriately, students can be given accommodations tailored to their individual learning needs. These often include more time to complete assignments, testing in a distraction free environment, use of an audio recorder, and shorter assignments. When possible, students are also taught learning behaviors such as note taking, organization, time management, and study skills.

Perhaps what is most important for parents and guardians to be familiar with is the Individuals with Disabilities Education Act (IDEA) of 2004. This act governs how schools provide services to people ages 3–21 with disabilities. To summarize a very long document, the gist is that parents have the right to expect a public school to provide appropriate accommodations for students diagnosed with a learning disability.

According to IDEA, if parents suspect their child has a learning disability, they can request the school to test the child and the school is required to do so. What is not outlined in the act is the timeline for the assessment. This means that most students wait months before an official assessment can be had. Parents can also get their child tested on their own and the school is required to consider the results of that assessment in their accommodations.

Note that a school is not required to agree with a private doctor's assessment. Once a diagnosis is received, the school is required to create an individualized education program (IEP) that specifies when, where, and how students' disabilities will be accommodated and their learning assessed. There are sections to outline teacher responsibilities, student responsibilities, and parent responsibilities that jointly facilitate student learning.

For example, teachers are responsible for providing accommodations as outlined in an IEP. A student may be responsible for evaluating the usefulness of said accommodations. Parents are responsible for communicating to the school anything that may affect a student's IEP (e.g., additional diagnoses, change of living environment, etc.). An IEP is only effective if the entire IEP team is in constant communication.

The IEP team includes the student (if age appropriate), parents, a regular education teacher, a special education teacher, an administrator, and someone qualified to interpret test results. Given that many public schools do not have certified special education teachers or school psychologists, this component of the act is rarely adhered to.

In reality, IEPs tend to be created by teachers and given to parents for their review and signature. As a parent, you have the right to be present and contribute to the creation of a learning plan for your child. IEPs are required to be reviewed annually, but more frequent revisions can be made at the written request of the parents. IEPs are also required to be made available to parents and teachers whenever requested.

If your child starts in a new school, be certain to bring the most recent copy of their IEP. This will be the guiding document until a new IEP can be developed at the new school. Because IEPs tend to be long, you should also be able to summarize the key components of the document: the diagnosis and the accommodations.

In some instances, accommodations for learning may include additional staff beyond the classroom teacher. Your child may receive a para professional who in severe cases attends every class and helps with classwork, or in other situations serves as a tutor. Children can also be placed in special education classes or programs. In the former, similar to gifted classes, students are pulled out of class to learn specific subjects in a more supportive learning environment.

Special education classes often have fewer students and multiple teachers who can provide individualized help to students. If students need help in three or more subject areas, they can be placed in a special education program. Placement in a special education program means that the special education teacher is their primary teacher though they may attend elective courses (also called "specials") with mainstream students. Less common, a school may choose to mix special education and mainstream students in inclusive classrooms.

When making educational decisions for a child with a learning disability or disorder, be sure to consider the type of support offered by a school. It can be helpful to talk to other parents at the school about their experiences creating and revising IEPs. It is also perfectly acceptable to "interview" teachers and administrators about their special education programs, their knowledge of IDEA, and their ability and willingness to adhere to policies.

TAKEAWAYS

As a parent, there are dozens of things to consider when choosing a school for your child. If your child's brain works a little differently than most, it adds an extra layer of complexity to educational decision-making. In many ways, having an intellectually gifted student is more difficult than having one with learning disabilities because the K-12 world hasn't quite figured out what to do in the rare cases of giftedness.

If you are considering a gifted program or school, be sure to do your research before applying to the program. The mere title of "gifted" does not mean it will meet your child's needs. Review the admissions criteria, talk to the teachers, and observe a few classes. This will help you ascertain if it is a good fit for your child both cognitively and socially.

Though there are gifted programs in most schools, they are not designed for children with extremely high IQs or with unique talent in a specific area. If your local school district doesn't offer a program like Horizons, there is still much you can do to supplement your child's need for academic rigor.

The first thing to do is to create a supportive learning environment in the home. Many gifted students feel out of place not only academically, but also socially. It can be hard for children to maintain social relationships with peers when their mind sometimes acts like an adult's. Home should be a safe haven for gifted youth who may experience ostracism from peers who find them "weird." An environment of acceptance is critical for the emotional well-being of gifted youth.

Another important thing to do is to ensure your child is getting the mental stimulation they need to remain engaged and interested in learning. Stimulation can look different for each child. Some children will be satisfied by having a tutor or going to a local learning center where they can play mentally challenging games. Other children might need more in-depth support such as after-school and summer programs for gifted youth.

Many colleges and universities offer such programs through their education departments. In the summer, the programs tend to be residential, offering students the opportunity to be surrounded by like-minded peers for at least a few months of the year. For children with domain-specific talents, consider enrolling them in a class or activity that utilizes their skills. This will provide individualized guidance toward strengthening their skills.

Students with learning disabilities also need individualized attention. As a parent, your first step is to be an advocate for your child. You should familiarize yourself with policies related to learning differences and ensure your child's school is adhering to such policies. Start small by observing your child's class to see if their teacher is able and willing to provide the necessary learning accommodations. If not, it is perfectly fine to request your child be moved to another classroom.

Sometimes, children just need a teacher who "speaks their language" and can explain concepts in a way aligned with how their brain works. It might also be beneficial if you spoke with teachers early in the year to explain your child's needs and request altered due dates for major projects or assignments.

Remember that academic accommodations are not just for school. You will need to make sure that, to all possible extents, those same accommodations exist in the home. Because the chief learning issue often involves processing, it is important that children have the time and space to do their schoolwork. Frustration is an inevitable part of the learning process for everyone, but for students with learning disabilities, it can become overwhelming.

Your job is to help alleviate some of the frustration that comes with learning disabilities. You can create a homework corner and quiet hours so your child works in a dedicated space during a dedicated time. For students with emotional disabilities, the consistency in their academic schedule will help lessen high stress levels.

You might also review good study habits, note taking, and organizational skills so your child's brain doesn't have to do any extra work while trying to learn difficult material. Encourage your child to take frequent breaks to give the brain a rest. Proper sleep and nutrition are also key to helping an overtaxed brain remain as healthy as possible.

REFERENCES

Charlotte Mecklenburg Schools. (2015). *Horizons Program*. Retrieved from: http://www.cms.k12.nc.us/cmsdepartments/ci/astd/horizons/Pages/default.aspx

Siegler, R. (1994). Cognitive variability: A key to understanding cognitive development. *Psychological Science*, 3(1), 1–5.

US Department of Education. (2015). Office of Special Education Programs. *Building the Legacy: IDEA 2004*. Retrieved from: http://idea.ed.gov/explore/home

Vocabulary to Know

Associated Words/Phrases	Definition
Domain general	Involving many parts of the brain; Encompassing broad, more global thinking
Domain specific	Involving specific parts of the brain; Encompassing specific topical thinking
Cognitive variability	Differences in how people think
Synaptogenesis	A process through which unused neural connections are shed and frequently used connections are strengthened
Norm-referenced tests	Tests that report how results compare to an average hypothetical test taker who is demographically similar to the test taker
Kaufman Test of Educational Achievement	Standardized assessment of reading, math, written language and oral language for PreK-12
Stanford-Binet	Standardized assessment of five cognitive abilities for ages 2-85
Iowa Test of Basic Skills	Standardized assessment of content knowledge for grades K-8
Organic	Relating to natural brain functioning
Information processing	What the brain does with information
Dyslexia	Difficulty identifying speech sounds and how they relate to letters and words; Emerges as reading difficulties
Dysgraphia	Difficulty with writing abilities, most often handwriting
Dyspraxia	A neurological disorder that impairs cognitive abilities and motor skills
Dyscalculia	Difficulty understanding numbers and the relationships between numbers
Dysphasia/Aphasia	A language disorder affecting the ability to speak
Anxiety Disorder	A group of mental illnesses involving extreme emotional states; Often a result of organic and environmental influences
Attention Deficit Disorder	Difficulty sustaining and dividing attention for long periods of time
Attention Deficit Hyperactive Disorder	Difficulty sustain and dividing attention for long periods of time in addition to impulsivity and hyperactive behavior
Response to Intervention (RTI)	A multi-tiered process used to identify and support learning needs
Individualized Education Program	An educational learning plan designed for students with unique learning needs
Inclusive classrooms	Classrooms with traditional students and students with unique learning needs

Figure 5.1

Chapter Six

Identity Development ... In All of Its Forms

I worry about my child being the "only" in their class.
—Father of a transgender son

Now that we've talked about the developmental changes that children go through in a somewhat similar fashion, it's time to shift our attention to aspects of development children undergo in different ways. These differences between children are why one school can be great for your niece and be an awful fit for your mentee. In this chapter we consider how differences in children's racial, language, and sexual identities affect their daily schooling experiences.

Identity is all about who we are and how we see ourselves. Children begin to construct a *self-concept* during middle childhood, but don't really define a personal identity until adolescence. In 1966, developmental psychologist James Marcia suggested that identity formation occurs through two processes: exploration and commitment.

Exploration is when adolescents purposefully think about their *future selves.* During this process teenagers think a lot about the career they want, if and when they want to start a family, and where they'd like to live. To map out such detailed goals, teens must pause and reflect on their own upbringing including family values, religion, political affiliation, and other factors that influence individual decision-making.

Commitment comes after adolescents have explored their identity options. They may now have a definitive career in mind and be adamant that they never want to have kids. More important, they begin to make plans to achieve their goals, which may involve a lot of negotiation with parents if their goals are not aligned with their parents' goals for them.

Depending upon where teens are in the exploration and commitment processes, Marcia identified four patterns of identity development:

1. *Identity diffusion*—Teens are not exploring possible identities and have not committed to any particular identity.
2. *Foreclosure*—Teens have not explored possible identities but have nevertheless committed to an identity. Usually they are adopting the goals others have for them.
3. *Moratorium*—Teens are actively exploring possible identities but have not committed to anything.
4. *Identity achievement*—Teens have gone through exploration and are committed to an identity based upon how well it aligns with personal values and interests.

It is important to remember that adolescents go through this process for many aspects of their identity. In other words, identity is not a single characteristic. People have professional identities, political identities, social identities, racial identities, and sexual identities, among many others. Each of these is a single characteristic of a person that, when combined, creates a *self-perception.*

As a parent you may not agree with all of your child's chosen identities. In fact, it is expected that parents and teens will have conflict during both the exploration and commitment phases of identity development. Conversations that are supportive and open-minded go a long way in helping your teen embrace life choices that align with how they feel about themselves and how they see themselves. Forcing your choices on your child may lead to a mistrustful parent-child relationship.

Racial/Ethnic identity development. Especially important during identity development is a child's racial or ethnic identity formation. In years past, people's racial classification was imposed upon them based on society's interpretation of their skin color. With more mixed-race families, children are now undergoing more complex racial identity development processes and are choosing how they would like to be classified.

While we don't have a mixed-race identity development model yet, William Cross did develop a racial identity development model for people of color. While Marcia's model is categorical, Cross's model is a stage model because he believes racial identity development is a process. He described five stages that children of color go through to develop a positive perception of themselves:

1. *Pre-encounter stage*—Children of color internalize the dominant negative views of racial and ethnic minorities. They try to assimilate into white culture by adopting the beliefs and values of dominant groups. They may also distance themselves from other people of color.

2. *Encounter stage*—An event or series of events forces children of color to acknowledge the impact of racism on their lives. They begin to accept that no matter what they do or say, they can never be white.
3. *Immersion/emersion stage*—Children learn about their racial and ethnic origins. They associate with people from their own ethnic group, avoid whiteness, and unlearn internalized stereotypes.
4. *Internalization stage*—Children become secure in their identity and no longer distance themselves from whiteness. They work to establish meaningful relationships with white people, while maintaining relationships with other racial minorities.
5. *Commitment stage*—Children of color are committed to improving the experiences of racial and ethnic minorities. They may become socially or politically active in community organizations.

Cross believes that children will begin this process as soon as they have an encounter experience. Such experiences are often negative, in which children are made to feel different because of their race or ethnicity. This happens a lot when a racial minority kid is the only child of color in the class or playgroup, so children who attend predominately white schools move through this process faster than children in racially diverse schools.

Because the encounter experience is likely to happen when children are away from parents, it is important that parents help children (especially if they are young) work through their emotional reactions. In order to move to the next stage of racial identity development, and ultimately to a committed racial identity, children must be emotionally and mentally prepared to manage interracial interactions.

Too often children are made to feel isolated because of their race or ethnicity, and this isolation can have negative effects on their academic performance. Being the only racial minority in a classroom often means that the student is looked upon as the spokesperson for an entire race. No person, especially a child, should be asked to represent the values and beliefs of an entire body of people when they themselves are still figuring out their own values and beliefs.

This self-exploration is especially difficult for racial minority students because the school curriculum does not often present diverse perspectives. Many students struggle to remain engaged when they rarely see people who look like them in their textbooks. Imagine how difficult it is to feel as though academic content is relevant to your personal identity when your identity (or identities) is never talked about or acknowledged at school.

Children's racial identity is an important consideration in their education because it affects how they are treated at school. Many racially and ethnically diverse students do not have the *cultural capital* many of their white classmates possess. Decades of research has found that African American students in particular have behaviors, styles of dress, and manners of speaking that are contrary to the white middle-class values that shape school functioning.

When a child brings different *cultural norms* into the classroom, the result is often *cultural dysynchrony*. If a child comes to school with a different—often opposing—idea of what constitutes good behavior, appropriate dress, or academic language, the child is likely to be punished for breaking school rules. Students of color are the ones most often suspended, expelled, and physically restrained in schools.

The differences in academic expectations can also result in students of color being viewed as academically delayed. Racial minorities are overrepresented in special education classes and underrepresented in gifted classes. They are also more likely than white students to be given a diagnosis of a learning disability or emotional disorder. Once given a label, students are tracked into lower-level classes, often without the opportunity to rejoin mainstream classes.

There is a lot of research about the tendency of teachers to view students of color from a *deficit-based perspective*. This negative perception can result in lower academic expectations, overly punitive punishments, and poor family–school relationships. The *achievement gap* between white students and students of color has led education reform advocates to seek pedagogical methods and curricula that are inclusive: focused on *equity* instead of *equality*.

Language identity development. The companion piece to ethnic/racial identity development is language development. Our first language—sometimes called our heritage language—is largely determined by our cultural identity, which encompasses our ethnic identity. This is not to say that if you speak Mandarin, you identify as Chinese. What it means is that a person who identifies as Chinese is more likely to speak Mandarin than someone who identifies as German. Our racial and ethnic identities often dictate our heritage language.

But many US public school students do not consider English their heritage language. Nine percent of students are nonnative English speakers and thus label Spanish, Arabic, Swahili, Mandarin, French, or another language as their first language. If they are not fluent in English, they are given the label of an English language learner (ELL) and are subject to the experiences that come with this imposed identity.

Because our schools are primarily English-only, English is the target language. When students are not fluent in English, they are often viewed as intellectually deficient (despite the fact that many nonnative English speakers are multilingual—an impressive cognitive feat). In many ways, the double minority status of being a person of color and/or immigrant and of being a nonnative English speaker can make school a hostile place for 9 million ELL students.

As if this wasn't enough, ELL students also face more academic demands than English speaking students. In order to become proficient in English, they must participate in bilingual education programs while simultaneously learning traditional academic content in English-only classrooms. Imagine learning chemistry in Italian while you take a beginner's Italian class. It is almost impossible to learn through a language without command of that language.

The natural response is to, of course, teach and test ELL students in their heritage language until they become fluent in English. But so few teachers are multilingual that it is rare for a school district to offer instruction in languages other than English. Given that reality, public schools most often rely on one of the three models to simultaneously teach students English and the academic content necessary to be successful in a testing-heavy educational climate.

Bilingual education. Within bilingual education there are two models for fostering English language development: additive and subtractive.

An additive model of language education is about adding English to students' repertoire of languages. English language learning is taught by helping students make connections between their heritage language and English. In other words, teachers capitalize on students' existing language abilities to help them learn a new language. The goal of additive language education is continued fluency in the heritage language and emerging fluency in the second language.

The primary way schools enact additive bilingualism is through dual immersion programs. A dual immersion program is exactly what it sounds like. In order for all students, including English speaking students, to learn a second language, *language majority* and *language minority* students are integrated in the same classroom and taught two languages.

If done properly, students receive equal amounts of time learning a new language and refining their skills in their first language. Critics of dual immersion programs doubt that teachers are always able to balance instruction and will spend more time teaching their own heritage language. Further, many people believe that dual immersion programs can be a waste of time for English speaking students who can refine their English skills in a Language Arts class.

Proponents of separate English and second language instruction often endorse a subtractive model of language education. Subtractive models are focused 100% on English language learning. All instruction and all assignments are done in English to help students be immersed in English. Some schools scaffold students' English immersion by beginning the program with instruction in a first language and slowly transitioning to English-only instruction.

The goal of subtractive language models is for students to stop using their first language and write, speak, and read solely in English when at school. Psychologists call it subtractive because this pedagogical approach limits children's exposure to their first language, often resulting in them losing those language skills. While the outcome of additive models is often bilingualism, the outcome of subtractive models is English fluency.

Education policies ebb and flow with respect to which of these models is most used. Psychologists heavily endorse the additive model due to its alignment with brain functioning and brain development. Educators tend to endorse the subtractive model because it is more efficient and more feasible. Further, because there are no policies that allow translation during standardized testing, students need to be fluent in English to successfully pass state tests.

But there are negative psychosocial effects of losing a heritage language in favor of English fluency. When children stop speaking their first language, research suggests that their self-esteem lowers and their relationships with family members become strained. Our language identity is far more than the words we speak; it is the way in which we engage our cultural history. Too many children are asked to forego their cultural identity in favor of an academic identity.

Sexual identity development. Perhaps the most troubling aspects of identity development for psychologists are children's sexual identities. With little research on sexuality prior to the early 1990s, psychologists took for granted that sexual identity occurred in much the same way as any other developmental process: through a blend of nature and nurture. It was assumed that most people were *heterosexual* and followed traditional US *binary gender* norms.

In the last decade, however, it has become clear that there are far more people who do not identify as heterosexual and who do not conform to the male-female dichotomy than previously thought. Slowly but surely, our language is catching up to the many ways people view their own gender and construct romantic relationships.

Psychologists are beginning to realize the importance of Marcia's exploration and commitment phases to the development of gender and sexual identities. There are no commonly accepted models for gender identity development, but the strongest hypothesis is that the more children are free to explore diverse activities and people, the less likely they are to conform to strict male-female gender norms.

For example, we talked in Chapter 1 about girls liking princesses and boys preferring action figures. There is no data that says these preferences are innate. In fact, there are tons of data that suggest these preferences are learned. Girls wear dresses because they see women wearing dresses. Boys have short hair because men have short hair.

It is not a far stretch then to think about the effect of environmental exposure on children's beliefs about romantic relationships. If children only ever see male-female relationships, they will think that is what is "right." But when children observe male-male or female-female relationships, they are more likely to explore a same-sex relationship.

This does not mean that children of homosexual parents will be gay or lesbian. Research continues to confirm that sexuality is more genetic than environmental. What it does mean is that children will be more likely to explore their own sexual preferences if they are raised in an environment that supports such exploration.

Indeed, the best model of sexual identity development we have right now underscores the importance of a supportive environment to the development of a healthy sexual identity. Richard Troiden's four-stage model focuses on adolescents' desire to be self-coherent. According to Troiden, people do not fully develop their sexual identity until they are comfortable expressing their identity in public social settings.

The complexities of sexuality are highly controversial and many members of the *LGBTQIA* community disagree with Troiden's views on sexual identity development. Many queer people state that they've always been aware of their sexual identity and it did not require elaborate exploration to accept their sexuality. As psychologists and sociologists conduct more studies, we will certainly have alternative models of sexual identity development.

LGBTQIA students. But when it comes to educational decision-making, it matters less how one comes to have sexual preferences than how one navigates the expression of those preferences. Especially in middle and high school when children begin to explore romantic relationships, children's gender and sexual identities can have a huge impact on their interpersonal relationships, which affect academic achievement.

Psychologists and educators are just beginning to understand the experiences of LGBTQIA students in schools because many students do not feel comfortable or safe discussing their sexual identity and the experiences they have because of it. The incidents of school bullying, aided by social media, are at an all-time high in US public schools. The majority of students who experience bullying identify as queer or are thought to be queer by classmates.

A 2013 study on the experiences of LGBTQIA students conducted by the Gay, Lesbian, and Straight Education Network (GLSEN) found that

55% of LGBT students said they feel unsafe at school because of their sexual orientation and 38% said they feel unsafe because of their gender expression. Over half of the students who experienced harassment said they did not feel comfortable reporting it to school staff, and of those who did, 62% said nothing was done to address the harassment.

LGBTQIA students were found to be three times more likely than heterosexual students to miss school, have lower grade point averages, and higher levels of depression. The same study found four things that helped make students feel safer at school: a gay-straight alliance (GSA) at the school, LGBT-inclusive curricula, supportive teachers, and comprehensive antibullying policies.

As of academic year 2015–2016, it's become more common for schools to implement gender neutral language policies where "he/him/his" and "she/her/hers" are replaced with "they/them/theirs." Some teachers are making it a point to ask students their preferred gender pronouns instead of assuming it; even though someone may look how society says boys should look, he may not want to be referred to as male.

Though odd to many over the age of 25, a shift in language goes a long way to making people feel accepted and respected. If children are focused on altering their gender expression or hiding their sexuality from peers and teachers because they are afraid of not being accepted, they have little cognitive and emotional resources left to meaningfully engage in their education. Like all aspects of identity, gender and sexuality are self-determined but should be socially supported.

TAKEAWAYS

Students bring far more than their academic experiences into the classroom every day. One of the reasons teachers consider themselves social workers, counselors, and second parents is because they spend 7 hours a day helping children find a balance between their personal self and their academic self.

This is not always an easy task, because children's personal identity characteristics are sometimes misaligned with the academic norms of public school. Ethnic and racial minority children must contend with the fact that their cultural practices are rarely represented in the curriculum, at school events, or by teachers. The absence of personal relevance in the day-to-day experiences of millions of students can cause academic disengagement and underachievement.

For students whose first language is not English, the erasure of their heritage language in subtractive models of language education is a continuing problem in schools. Many English language learners must contend with the burden of an additional curriculum of English instruction that makes school cognitively exhausting. The difficulties in negotiating cultural identities and academic expectations cause high stress for students acting as cultural brokers.

But even for students who are perhaps members of the cultural and language majority, school can be a difficult and uncomfortable place. Sexual minority students are bullied more than any other demographic of student in public schools. Like ethnic and racial minorities, LGBTQIA students rarely see their lived experiences reflected in academic curriculum and also experience disproportionate rates of disciplinary referrals and consequent academic failure.

Unlike for students with learning disabilities or physical impairments, there are no federal or state policies that dictate how to ensure that marginalized youth receive equitable education opportunities. Individual districts and schools are left to figure it out for themselves and, unsurprisingly, many students fall through the cracks.

The inequitable educational experiences of diverse students are certainly a structural problem that cannot be solved by a few well intentioned teachers. But parents can do their best to make sure a district provides and requires special trainings or workshops for school personnel on diversity-related issues. Checking out schools' family engagement programs is another way to ascertain how the school views issues of difference.

School policies about the dress code and bullying can provide insight into what cultural norms, perspectives, and behaviors are viewed as "normal" and which are subject to punishment. Parents should also request a copy of the yearlong curriculum (and lesson plans if available) to see if and how specific demographic groups are included in the content.

So often parents are concerned with ensuring that their child has a good teacher, they forget to investigate the context in which and through which learning occurs. The best teacher in the world cannot overcome discriminatory or biased curricula, programs, or policies. It is best to work top-down to ensure that your child is receiving a high quality social and emotional experience to facilitate academic learning.

REFERENCES

Carol, L. Y. (2009). Language maintenance and language loss in first language. *U.S.-China Foreign Language*, 7(7), 10–16.

Cohens, J., and Wickens, C. M. (2015). Speaking English and the loss of a heritage language. *Teaching English as a Second or Foreign Language*, 18(4), 1–24.

Cross, W. (1991). *Shades of Black: Diversity in African American identity.* Philadelphia, PA: Temple University Press.

Erickson, E. (1968). *Identity: Youth and crisis.* New York, NY: W.W. Norton

GLSEN. (2013). Retrieved from: http://www.glsen.org/article/2013-national-school-climate-survey

Krashen, S. (2000). Bilingual education, the acquisition of English, and the retention and loss of Spanish. In A. Roca (Ed.), *Research on Spanish in the U.S.: Linguistic issues and challenges.* Somerville, MA: Cascadilla Press.

Marcia, J. E. (1980). Identity in adolescence. In J. Adelson (Ed.), *Handbook of adolescent psychology.* New York, NY: Wiley.

Troiden, R. R. (1993). The formation of homosexual identities. In L. D. Garnets and D. C. Kimmel (Eds.), *Psychological perspectives on lesbian and gay male experiences* (pp. 191–217). New York, NY: Columbia University Press.

Vocabulary to Know	
Associated Words/Phrases	Definition
Self-concept	A person's overall belief about who they are and what they can do
Future self	Who someone wants to become
Self-perception	How a person views themselves
Cultural capital	Non-financial social assets that promote social mobility
Cultural norms	Shared expectations and rules that guide behavior of people within social groups
Cultural dysynchrony	Misalignment of cultural norms between social groups
Tracking	Placing students in ability groups based upon prior achievement
Mainstream classroom	Traditional classrooms without special instructional techniques
Defict-based teaching	Teaching that assumes children lack desired knowledge or skills
Achievement gap	The difference in standardized test scores between genders and racial and economic groups
Equity	Giving each child what they individually need
Equality	Giving each child the same thing
English language learner	A student whose first language is not English
Target language	A language a person intends to learn
Language majority	People who speak the dominant language in a society
Language minority	People whose first language is not the dominant language in a society
Academic identity	How a person thinks of themselves as a student in the context of school
Sexual identity	How a person thinks of themselves based upon to whom they are physically and sexually attracted
Gender binary	The classification of sex and gender as male or female
LGBTQIA	Lesbian, Gay, Bisexual, Transgender, Queer, Intersex, Asexual/Ally
Queer	A self-identification that is outside gender and sexual societal norms
Gender expression	The ways in which people manifest their gender identity
Cultural brokers	People who bridge the gap between different cultural groups
Sexual minority	A person whose sexual identity is different from the sexual identities of most of the people around them

Figure 6.1

Part II

HOW PEOPLE LEARN

Now that we know what happens in development, we can focus our attention on what happens in the classroom. More specifically, we can think about what should happen in the classroom because of development.

Part II is all about the psychological theories that (should) guide classroom practices. Each chapter begins with an overview of a particular psychological theory developed by psychologists whose names may be familiar by now. Jean Piaget, Lev Vygotksy, Ivan Pavlov, and B. F. Skinner resurface in the coming pages. You will also be introduced to Abraham Maslow and Carl Rogers who pioneered humanistic counseling and teaching practices.

After reviewing the origins of Constructivism, Humanism, Socioculturalism, and Behaviorism, I discuss how and why each psychological theory transferred into the realm of education. I spend a good amount of time discussing how sometimes theories don't translate to practice easily, so what happens in a school is not always aligned with its foundational theory. For you to better understand how psychological theories can become instructional methods, each chapter includes a section on "what it looks like in the classroom." In this section I clearly state the overall learning objective of an educational model before describing the classroom practices that support the objective.

Classroom practices include not only what teachers and students do, but also the social and emotional contexts in which learning happens. I will review mundane but very important things like how desks are organized and common rules that structure the classroom environment. Perhaps more interesting is the discussion of the teacher's role in the classroom, the types of assignments given, and procedures for evaluating student learning.

Given what you now know about child development, the sections describing the ideal student for each model may or may not be illuminating. I make clear that certain learning goals, teaching methods, and assessment criterion are best aligned with specific developmental abilities and personality traits. I also discuss what parents are expected to do to support children's learning, so that you can determine if this model is good for you too.

Even with all of that information, it can be hard to envision what a school would look like and if it would be a good fit for your child or not. To help clarify how psychological theory can become educational practice, each chapter includes a description of a US school that effectively implements a particular model of education.

By the end of Part II you will be able to synthesize what you know about development with what you know about schools to make the best educational decisions for your family. You will have a firm understanding of which pedagogical techniques are appropriate for which ages, personalities, and academic talents. Most of all, you will understand the cyclical nature of development and learning and why it's so important to recognize that learning really does happen from the inside-out.

Chapter Seven

Constructivism

I'm a constructivist teacher. I want my students to learn how to think critically.
—Middle school science teacher

OVERVIEW

Pedagogical Model: *Constructivism*
Origin: *Psychology*
Learning Goal: *Thinking skills*
Best for:
Ages: *11+*

> Kids who are: *Social; Creative; Inquisitive; Inventive; Independent; Intellectually Gifted; Experiencing processing-related learning disabilities*
> Parents who: *Can accommodate expensive projects; Can invest time into helping with long-term assignments*

PSYCHOLOGICAL CONSTRUCTIVISM

Constructivism is one of the most misunderstood and misused terms in K-12 schools. Often you hear teachers describe themselves as "constructivist" teachers because their learning goals are grounded in *self-discovery*. As such, constructivist teaching is often equated with *inquiry-based learning*, *experiential learning*, and *project-based learning*. While those methods do reflect many of the tenants of constructivism, there is no such thing as constructivist teaching.

Grounded in the cognitive psychological work of Jean Piaget, constructivism is an epistemological theory about how people learn. Piaget developed his theories after studying his own children for close to 20 years. After meticulous data collection, he devised a theory of child development grounded in four stages: sensorimotor (birth–2 years), preoperations (2–7 years), concrete operations (7–10 years), and formal operations (10+).

Piaget described development as shifts in how children think about the world based upon their interactions with objects in their environment. While Piaget observed how his own children experimented with toys, household items, rocks, and other objects, psychologists have developed controlled experiments to replicate Piaget's findings.

For example, in experiments with young children, kids ages 4 and 5 are shown two graham crackers: one for the experimenter and one for themselves. They are asked how many graham crackers they each have and if they have the same amount. Four- and 5-year-olds correctly indicate that each person has one graham cracker, and yes, they both have the same amount.

Then the experimenter picks up her graham cracker and snaps it in two. She then asks the child again if they both have the same amount of graham crackers. Children in the preoperational stage of development will say no, that the experimenter now has more crackers because she has two. Children in concrete operations will explain that they still have the same amount of crackers even though it appears as though the experimenter has more.

This is what Piaget called Conservation of Number—an understanding that even if an object's appearance changes, the number of those objects has not changed. Piaget argued that it was through playing with objects that kids come to understand such truths. In other words, Piaget believed that children construct their understandings of the world as they interact with their environment.

His theory is grounded in his belief that development leads to learning (remember this from Chapter 2?), so in many ways Piaget's ideas about how development happens were limited. Piaget outlined three rules for constructivist learning:

1. Learning requires normal brain functioning
2. Learning happens in isolation
3. There are no universal truths

The first of his rules is implied in most theories of how children develop and learn. Because such theories are derived from extended studies of children with normal brain functioning, the results of the studies are applicable only to that population. In constructivism in particular, this rule is especially important because Piaget believed that without proper brain functioning, children might never be able to understand principles like Conservation of Number.

With a healthy brain leading the way, Piaget did not believe that children need assistance to learn. He believed that the brain is self-teaching and that all children have the capacity to learn as long as they've developed the proper brain structures. In one of his most famous speeches, Piaget describes how a 5-year-old's brain is not developed enough to learn advanced algebra, but by age 11 or 12 the brain would be able to support complicated mathematical processes.

Because Piaget didn't have the technology we have now, he couldn't be specific about brain development and what he meant by brain structures. Without MRI machines and other neuroimaging techniques, it's amazing that he was able to accurately hypothesize that higher-order skills such as logic and reasoning do indeed emerge in early adolescence as the frontal lobe develops. This is why your 12-year-old takes pre-algebra and your 7-year-old doesn't.

Piaget's final rule is not as well supported by neuroscience. He believed that because learning happens in isolation, everyone can and will interpret the world differently. We now know that people's brains develop the same cognitive skills around the same time, leading most people to make similar conclusions about principles of number, physics, and geometry.

But Piaget was correct in stating that people's interpretations of the world are merely working hypotheses. Theories like Overlapping Waves (discussed in Chapter 4) support the idea that as children have more experiences in more settings, they refine what they know and are better able to justify their conclusions. For Piaget, then, learning is not what you know; it is your ability to reason about what you know.

EDUCATIONAL CONSTRUCTIVISM

Shortly after Piaget developed his theory of constructivism, it came under heavy critique because it ignored the importance of social interaction. After all, human beings are social beings and no one exists in a bubble of isolation. In response to the emergence of other educational-developmental theories (namely socioculturalism, discussed in Chapter 9), theorists calling themselves neo-Piagetians adapted the theory to account for social influences on learning.

Neo-Piagetians created a new theory that acknowledged the role of race, gender, family structure, and other social variables in shaping how people learn. They called this theory, *social constructivism*.

The primary difference between constructivism and social constructivism is that the latter accepts the existence of social knowledge, or shared beliefs among a group of people. Numerous studies demonstrate that people with shared social traits (like religious affiliation) tend to have similar ideas about how the world works.

Those studies uncovered that a person's social identity creates a set of experiences that others with the same social identity share. It makes sense then that people who go to the same church and have similar religious experiences end up having the same religious beliefs and values.

Similarly, when placed in a classroom, social constructivism capitalizes on the shared experiences of students in the same class. Because a class of first graders learns single digit subtraction together, they all come to the same conclusion that any number minus zero leaves that number unchanged. The students may use different methods to experiment with zero, but they all end up in the same place: with the absolute truth that zero is the same thing as nothing.

Despite the influence of shared social experiences on cognition, neo-Piagetians do not retract their belief that learning happens in isolation. Instead, they extended the theory to acknowledge that learning can also happen through social interaction. It is social constructivism then, not pure constructivism, that has a place in our schools.

What it looks like in the classroom. Social constructivist classrooms have a clear learning objective: to help students develop *critical thinking* skills.

Teachers act as educational guides who teach students how to evaluate their own thought processes. Because social constructivism is about students learning by interacting with their environment, teachers are responsible for establishing a classroom that facilitates inquiry and reflection.

Instead of a heavy reliance on textbooks or worksheets, social constructivist teachers endorse student-centered learning. The goal is for students to learn about a topic with minimal direct instruction from the teacher. To get students started, teachers will provide students with the basic information necessary to complete a predesigned task. The information can come from books, a video, a guest speaker, or sometimes a field trip.

Teachers then present an activity that is designed to help students uncover their thinking about a particular topic, even if it is unfamiliar to the students. This activity can be as simple as a think-pair-share activity where students individually reflect on a topic, pair with a classmate, and share their ideas before reporting verbally to the entire class.

But it can also be as complex as asking students to role play the signing of the Emancipation Proclamation before ever learning about it.

Such an activity encourages students to tap into what they already know to formulate hypotheses about something they don't know—the core of constructivist learning.

Teachers help students explore their thinking through a variety of ways. It is common for young students to use manipulatives and for older students to do experiments to develop hypotheses about how things work. Some teachers also encourage playing music or dancing when students have a difficult time with words. Other activities may involve trips to nontraditional educational settings like a hospital, community center, or museum.

Because critical thinking is the goal of social constructivism, most learning tasks are designed to directly challenge students' preconceived ideas about how the world works. Learning materials are chosen with the intent to provoke disagreement and discussion among students. Desks are moved around to encourage students to work with different people who are thinking about course material in different ways.

The assessment of learning is therefore all about students' justification of their beliefs. Rather than multiple choice tests or the standard essay, many assessments include a project where students create something that demonstrates the evolution of their understanding. The grading of such a project is not based upon artistic talent, but on students' ability to communicate their ideas in a logical and clear manner.

Students are given freedom to choose a format that works best for them. Some students might choose to write a traditional paper while others may make a video. An effective social constructivist teacher is able to look beyond the presentation of the content to truly evaluate the substance of the content.

This can be tricky, because in many cases there is no right or wrong answer. Teachers may be reluctant to tell students what the learning goal for a particular lesson is because they do not want to influence students' thinking; however, new education policies now require teachers to cite specific learning objectives for each lesson.

This rigidity means students don't have as much flexibility in the outcomes of their thinking as social constructivist theory intends. But good social constructivist teachers do their best to evaluate if the students' interpretation is "valid" while also ensuring they meet learning targets.

For some parents, the ambiguity and apparent subjectivity of assessment is off-putting. The lack of clear instructions for how to do something can also be challenging for some students. The outcome in such a classroom is paradoxically the process. Teachers are hoping to foster higher-order thinking skills such as application and transfer, synthesis, evaluation/critique, inductive/deductive/hypothetical reasoning, and logic, among others.

Interestingly, these cognitive skills are all milestones Piaget said would emerge in the final stage of development, formal operations. It therefore makes sense that a pedagogical approach grounded in Piaget's theory of constructivism would have a goal of cognitive development.

For whom social constructivism is best. Social constructivism only works if students are able to think complexly about academic content. The unstructured nature of the learning process may be difficult for kids who need direct instruction and explicit rules to guide their learning. Without the proper experiences that according to constructivist theory incite development, social constructivism is not an effective model of learning for kids under age 8.

What also matters is a child's natural disposition for learning. One's disposition includes one's temperament and personality, academic interests and goals, and the ways one learns best. When we think about personalities, social constructivist classrooms are best suited for socially flexible kids. An activity-based classroom means that children will need to be okay working in various contexts and in a sometimes noisy environment.

If your child has a preference for working alone in silence, this doesn't mean a social constructivist class won't work for them. Students who excel in these classrooms are those who can be as successful working independently as they are working in a group of five.

Social constructivism is not the best model of schooling for shy children who may struggle to find their voice in what can appear to be a chaotic setting. The emphasis on self-discovery means that students must be willing to take the initiative to ask questions and willingly share ideas. Similarly, domineering children who always have to be in charge may find it difficult to step back, listen to others, and take feedback graciously.

Successful students in social constructivist classes have good communication skills. They speak clearly, ask questions, and listen attentively. The constant communication means there is a lot going on, so students need to be well-behaved and trustworthy. While no child is perfectly behaved all the time, teachers in social constructivist classes expect students to be self-motivated and self-monitoring.

Beyond personality, children's *learning style* matters a lot in a social constructivist class. Because of the emphasis on process instead of product, kids whose primary objective is learning—not being the best—will do well in this setting. These kids possess what educational psychologists call *academic venturesomeness*—a desire and willingness to try something new. If your child is preoccupied with grades and class rank, a social constructivist class is probably not the best choice.

In fact, high achieving students in this framework are those who are not at all concerned about the product of their efforts. In everyday life, these are children who often begin an activity with no clear goal in mind. Their seemingly laidback attitude can drive parents crazy, but this may be what makes them especially successful in the right school.

Kids who *think outside the box* are well-suited for social constructivist education. Their ideas may not always be conventional, but they are unique. These children like to make up games or stories, invent things, and are very detail oriented in their creations.

In educational terms, they are *creative*. In psychological terms, they are *novel*. These are kids who solve problems in ways you'd never imagine, or who can take a random sampling of items and create something useful and original. In a classroom where the primary goal is creating meaning, innovation is highly encouraged.

Tactile or *kinesthetic learning* is the chief method of engagement in social constructivism. This doesn't mean your child needs to be artistically or mechanically inclined to do well. It means that your child learns best when they are physically moving. These children act things out, talk with their hands, or draw and doodle. Kids who are drawn to athletics or performing arts tend to be kinesthetically inclined and may particularly enjoy being in a social constructivist classroom where they are welcome to move around.

This model of schooling is also good for children who've been identified as academically gifted (broadly or in a specific area). Students in social constructivist classes generally work at their own pace. This means that gifted children can work ahead without feeling pressure to slow down. They can also choose to delve more deeply into interesting topics because they are not restricted by grade-level textbooks or worksheets. This allows them to work toward their full potential.

Kids who experience certain types of learning disabilities may struggle in a social constructivist class. In particular, children with ADD/ADHD and any form of anxiety might find it difficult to navigate their learning in an unstructured environment. Conversely, students with processing disorders might actually find this classroom beneficial in helping them work through their thoughts and practice their expressive language skills.

A social constructivist model of education can in many ways be a catch-all because of its emphasis on cognitive development. Unlike other models of education, social constructivism explicitly facilitates growth of academic and social skills in a safe environment where everyone is being challenged to think "better," so there are no top students. This also means that children who don't have all of the aforementioned skills have the opportunity to develop them.

When looking for a social constructivist classroom within a traditional public school, pay attention to small details. These classrooms should be project-based and interdisciplinary in nature. They should also focus a lot on children's growth instead of the end result of their learning. Once found, the key to deciding if this style of education is right for your child is in being honest about their interest in, and capacity to, figure things out for themselves.

A REAL LIFE EXAMPLE: EXPERIENTIAL LEARNING SCHOOLS

Experiential learning dates back to the famous educational philosopher John Dewey. In 1938, he wrote a book titled *Experience and Education*, which is often cited as the first text to emphasize the importance of students' life experiences to their learning processes. Currently most experiential learning schools are private schools found in upper income areas, but increasingly they can also be found in urban areas, mostly marketed as charter schools.

Experiential schools are structured around a philosophy of education grounded in social constructivism. They are primarily focused on students making meaning from direct experiences. These experiences can happen within a traditional classroom setting or involve an international field trip around the globe. Indeed, many experiential learning (also called expeditionary learning) schools are characterized by their diverse study-abroad programs and student clubs.

Experiential education is often integrated into traditional schooling models, but in true experiential schools, students' out-of-class work forms the core of their learning. Echoing constructivist theory, experiential education is iterative. After an experience, students are both reflective and reflexive about their learning.

To be reflective, students think about the experience itself: how it was similar or different to prior experiences, what was exciting or challenging, and ways it could have been improved. To be reflexive, the emphasis is on analyzing one's self as the object of interest. Students answer questions such as how have I changed because of this experience? What have I learned? What did I rethink and why?

This leads to a change in thinking that influences their interpretation of the next experience. The emphasis on metacognition in experiential learning is a direct result of its constructivist origins.

The Association for Experiential Education (AEE) outlines the principles of experiential education on its website:

- Experiential learning occurs when carefully chosen experiences are supported by reflection, critical analysis, and synthesis.
- Experiences are structured to require the learner to take initiative, make decisions, and be accountable for results.
- Throughout the experiential learning process, the learner is actively engaged in posing questions, investigating, experimenting, being curious, solving problems, assuming responsibility, being creative, and constructing meaning.
- Learners are engaged intellectually, emotionally, socially, soulfully, and/ or physically. This involvement produces a perception that the learning task is authentic.
- The results of the learning are personal and form the basis for future experience and learning.
- Relationships are developed and nurtured: learner to self, learner to others, and learner to the world at large.
- The educator and learner may experience success, failure, adventure, risk-taking, and uncertainty, because the outcomes of experience cannot totally be predicted.
- Opportunities are nurtured for learners and educators to explore and examine their own values.
- The educator's primary roles include setting suitable experiences, posing problems, setting boundaries, supporting learners, insuring physical and emotional safety, and facilitating the learning process.
- The educator recognizes and encourages spontaneous opportunities for learning.
- Educators strive to be aware of their biases, judgments, and preconceptions, and how these influence the learner.
- The design of the learning experience includes the possibility to learn from natural consequences, mistakes, and successes.

A learning environment focused on self-awareness requires a curriculum with a lot of gray area. Students don't have textbooks, and instead rely more heavily on primary texts as their source of information. Assignments include a lot of perspective-taking and substantiating of opinions. True to constructivism, right and wrong answers are rare; providing evidence is of the utmost importance in an experiential school.

That evidence is most often found by engaging with people and content beyond the school walls. Many experiential schools have required internship and volunteer programs through which students interact with community organizations. Most classroom assignments require extensive research that synthesizes content knowledge with personal experiences.

While traditional classes are offered, there are opportunities for students to design their own course of study. For example, students in experiential schools can create a course centered on their work at a nonprofit organization or volunteering at a hospital. The students would work with site supervisors and their own teachers to find readings and identify projects that engender knowledge and skills of mutual benefit to the students and their community partner.

True to social constructivism, student evaluation at experiential schools is grounded in individual progress. There are no comparative metrics between students, and often they don't use a traditional A through F grading scale. Assessment includes narratives from teachers, community partners, and the students themselves about what they learned, how they learned, what they still need to learn, and how they plan to meet their learning goals. The focus is on whether students meet agreed upon expectations and clearly demonstrate their understanding of course material.

Experiential learning schools are becoming more popular as the United States searches for new approaches to education in our current era of reform. The emphasis on thinking skills is well aligned with Common Core State Standards, so many states are issuing charters for the creation of more experiential learning schools.

TAKEAWAYS

Social constructivist learning has its ups and downs. On the plus side, it is an interdisciplinary approach to teaching and learning, so children engage topics from multiple perspectives. Interdisciplinary teaching requires students to develop and employ thinking skills that facilitate the integration of ideas that sometimes conflict.

Critical thinking is something all schools say they do, but social constructivism is founded upon it. The level of engagement and participation required of students in a social constructivist class can foster a deeper interest in learning than is seen in traditional models of education.

One of the biggest flaws of social constructivism is its uniqueness. Kids who move from this model to a traditional classroom setting may find it hard to adapt to an individualistic learning environment where they don't experience the same level of social interaction. The emphasis on standardized testing may present difficulties as students adjust to new academic expectations.

Consequently, achievement levels may dip until students learn how to take tests and perhaps catch up on content that was not the primary learning target in their prior school. The transition to college may be especially difficult because most colleges are lecture-based and rely heavily on textbooks in lieu of other learning materials.

As parents, you are a primary component of your child's educational journey, but that role looks different in social constructivist schools. While many parents help their children with homework, you may not be able or asked to do so under this model. Because the focus is on students' thinking, parents are discouraged from engaging in direct instruction with their children.

While you can still quiz them on their spelling words, you may not understand the strategies they use to do three-digit multiplication. Parents of children in social constructivist classrooms are expected to support their child's learning by providing supplemental educational materials. This can be as simple as hiring a tutor, but can also be as difficult as helping your child find someone to interview about their experiences during the Vietnam War.

Because social constructivist teaching asks students to be creative, expect many trips to arts and crafts stores. You may also be asked to help with long-term projects not found in traditional public schools. For example, when learning about animal habitats, a teacher might ask students to do a case study of a single animal for the entire school year to observe its behaviors, eating habits, and living environment.

The catch is that in order to do such an extended study, the animal needs to be accessible on a daily basis. This means that families who don't live on a farm will need to purchase a pet—and no, it can't be a dog, cat, or fish because those animals are too common and may not present novel information to a learner.

While such an assignment requires an investment of the entire family, social constructivist schools tend to require very little parental volunteerism or participation at the school. This can be a plus for parents whose life context doesn't facilitate chaperoning field trips or reading to the class. Once your child is happily enrolled in a social constructivist school, parents' commitment to their learning is largely financial, not time.

If your child is inquisitive, creative, and tends to dance to the beat of their own drum, social constructivist models of schooling may be a good fit for them. This model is also good if your child is independent, thinks deeply about things, and likes to debate. Be cautious in choosing this type of classroom if your child is shy, prefers to work alone, or is motivated primarily by grades.

The financial commitment to support social constructivist learning can be a burden to parents, but it is worth reorganizing the budget if it enhances children's engagement in school. If you think social constructivism is right for your child and your family, begin exploring your options by seeking experiential learning schools in your area.

REFERENCES

Airasian, P. W., and Walsh, M. E. (1997). Constructivist cautions. *Phi Delta Kappan*, 444–449.

Association for Experiential Education. (2015). *What is experiential education?* Retrieved from: http://www.aee.org/what-is-ee

Dewey, J. (1938). *Experience and education*. New York, NY: Macmillan Press.

Gass, M. A., Gillis, H. L., and Russell, K. C. (2012). *Adventure therapy: Theory, research, and practice*. New York, NY: Routledge.

Gordon, M. (2009). Misuses and effective uses of constructivist teaching. *Teachers and Teaching: Theory and Practice*, 15(6), 737–746.

Piaget, J. (1964). Development and learning. In R. E. Ripple and V. N. Rockcastle (Eds.), *Piaget Rediscovered*, 7–20.

Vocabulary to Know Associated Words/Phrases	Definition
Self-discovery	Gaining knowledge or understanding about one's self
Inquiry-based learning	Instruction designed around asking/answering increasingly complex questions
Experiential learning	Instruction where students make meaning from direct experiences; learning through doing
Project-based learning	Interdisciplinary instructional approach in which students investigate real-world problems over extended periods of time
Social constructivism	Based upon principles of Constructivism; Children construct meaning with input from others
Cognition	The process of thinking
Critical thinking	Thinking involving higher-order skills; Focuses on application, synthesis and evaluation
Learning style	The ways in which people process information best (includes visual, auditory, kinesthetic/tactile)
Academic venturesomeness	Willingness to try new things
Thinking outside of the box	Thinking in uncommon or unusual ways
Creative	Innovative; often associated with artistry
Novel	New, unique, original
Kinesthetic learning	Also called tactile learning; learning involving physical movement
Expeditionary learning	Instruction derived from principles of Outward Bound; incorporates field trips and in-depth study of single topics; children construct meaning
Metacognition	Thinking about thinking

Figure 7.1

Chapter Eight

Humanism

School shouldn't just be about testing and academic smarts; it should educate the whole child.

—Mother of a 10-year-old

OVERVIEW

Pedagogical Model: *Humanism*
Origin: *Psychology*
Learning Goal: *Individualized growth*
Best for:
Ages: *All*

> Kids who are: *Shy or introverted; Experiencing developmental delays or learning disabilities; Intrinsically motivated; Curious; Have diverse interests*
> Parents who: *Have a lot of time to work with children; Value emotional well-being*

PSYCHOLOGICAL HUMANISM

Humanism emerged in the 1950s as a response to the focus of Behaviorism and *Psychoanalysis* on negative emotions. Humanists countered this rigid perspective by theorizing that all humans are innately good and live their lives figuring out how to be their best selves.

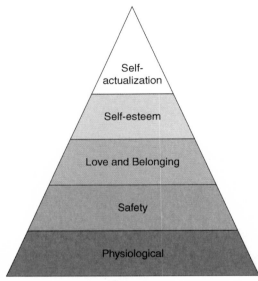

Figure 8.1

Abraham Maslow termed the realization of one's potential *self-actualization*. Maslow developed a theory about humans' *hierarchy of needs* to describe the process to achieve self-actualization. This theory is most often depicted visually as a pyramid with physiological needs at the bottom, social needs in the middle, and emotional needs at the top.

* *Physiological needs*—food, water, air, sleep
* *Safety needs*—shelter, safety, health care, employment
* *Social needs*—friendships, romantic relationships, community
* *Esteem needs*—self-worth, social acceptance
* *Self-actualization needs*—self-awareness, growth-oriented

Maslow stated that people cannot move to a higher level until they fulfill the needs of the prior level. Many psychologists criticize Maslow's theory because there is no evidence to support its hierarchical nature. For example, people can experience love and belonging without having access to health care or despite living in an unsafe neighborhood. Further, critics of this theory want a measurable definition of self-actualization that can be empirically studied.

Despite its pitfalls, Maslow's theory of humanism led Carl Rogers to create *client-centered therapy*. This new psychological counseling approach was about helping people connect with their *real selves* and create a *self-concept* based upon personal needs and desires on their journey toward self-actualization.

According to Rogers, in order to achieve self-actualization, people must have four things: unconditional positive self-regard, unconditional positive regard of others, a life free from physical, social, and emotional threats, and genuine relationships. Unlike other psychological theories, humanism acknowledges a person's simultaneous need for social participation and personal self-fulfillment. In the 1980s, Rogers' theories about the intersection of *self-worth*, *self-image*, and *ideal self* formed the basis for humanistic education.

HUMANISTIC EDUCATION

The learning objective of humanistic education is individual growth. Students are expected, and given support to, live up to their academic, social, and emotional potential. Humanist education is all about educating the *whole child*. While academic content is important, teachers also focus on developing students' *emotional intelligence*. Children in humanist schools develop strong self-awareness and good *self-regulated learning strategies*. As a result, they tend to have positive self-perceptions and a *growth mindset*.

Social relationships are at the core of humanistic learning. Teachers develop personal relationships with each student by being open about who they are, how they feel, and by valuing each student's expression of their needs. The rules in humanistic classroom relate to respect and honesty so the classroom climate can be free of emotional threats that might impede learning, and to a larger extent, self-actualization.

Discipline methods are grounded in aspects of client-centered therapy. Similar to *Restorative Justice* and *peer mediation*, conflicts are resolved by allowing each person to speak about how they were affected by others' behaviors. The goal is not to punish or penalize, but to facilitate positive social interactions in which everyone is aware of how their individual actions affect the larger community.

The thread of community extends into the curriculum. It is common for humanist schools to engage in interdisciplinary teaching where grade-level teachers collaborate to present related academic content at the same time across classes. For example, 9th graders might be learning about the free market in economics class, while simultaneously learning about European labor movements in history class and the environmental effects of industrialization in science class.

Pedagogy is centered on helping students understand concepts at both the macro and micro level by first painting a big picture and, later, relating concepts to students' personal lives. There is an emphasis on *skills-based learning* in humanistic education that empowers students to develop skills that allow them to use their knowledge for personal and social improvement. Many humanistic schools have community service requirements and a heavy focus on *community-based learning*.

There are also diverse course offerings including music, physical education, cooking, sewing, or gardening. Waldorf schools (reviewed in Chapter 1) are well known for their emphasis on life skill development alongside academic achievement. Because of their grounding in humanistic psychology, students are taught the skills necessary to meet their basic physiological needs within an environment that meets their safety, and their social and esteem needs.

Students' needs are explicitly stated in their *individualized learning plans* (ILPs). Here is where each student writes their personal goals for the day, week, month, semester, and/or year. In elementary school, teachers rely on students' past achievement, conversations with parents, and information from prior teachers to develop ILPs for each student.

Progress toward goals is measured through traditional assessments like homework and quizzes/tests, and through qualitative assessments such as oral or written self-reflections. Unlike other pedagogical models, humanism emphasizes students' agency in determining what counts as learning for them, so most assessment is grounded in whether students met the goals outlined in their ILP and how well students devise a learning plan to meet their goals.

Humanism may be the model of education that most closely mirrors its psychological roots. The positive classroom climate is a direct carryover from client-centered therapy that discourages criticism of one's self and of others. The individualized nature of humanistic learning underscores the psychological reality that people grow at different rates and want different things out of life.

For whom humanism is best. Children of all ages can benefit from a humanist classroom. With little emphasis on cognitive skills, humanistic learning is possible from Pre-K through college. It is an especially good learning environment for shy and timid children because the classroom climate is grounded in emotional safety. Humanism also works for introverted kids who may not feel comfortable participating in large groups but thrive on their own.

Humanism is appropriate for a wide range of academic ability levels. The self-pacing in humanism makes learning easier for children with learning disabilities or developmental delays. Individualized learning plans are focused on growth, not outcome, so every student is held to self-determined standards. Individualized attention helps children who need extra support excel in ways not possible in more traditional classrooms.

Because of the emphasis on positive social interactions, humanism is not suited for children who are competitive, need to be the center of attention, or have extreme behavioral disorders. Even though humanism is all about emotional support, children need foundational self-regulatory skills to be successful members of an emotionally delicate learning community. It would require a strong teacher to integrate aggressive children into the classroom.

A REAL LIFE EXAMPLE: P.A.I.D.E.I.A. COOPERATIVE SCHOOL IN ANCHORAGE, ALASKA

Humanist schools come in a variety of fashions. Most people point to Waldorf schools as the exemplar of humanism in public schools, but there are other variations of humanism in the classroom. *Cooperative schools* are an excellent example of the strong family-school partnership that supports humanistic education.

A cooperative school (or "co-op") functions as a collaboration between school personnel and parents/families. Most cooperative schools are founded by community members as an alternative to traditional schools. In the past, funding for cooperative schools came largely from private donors and religious organizations. With the popularity of charter schools, many co-ops are now charter schools whose funding comes in part from private corporations.

Parents at co-ops often constitute the governing body of the school. They decide on curriculum, participate in teacher and staff hiring, and in many cases provide instruction on a regular basis. Most co-ops are elementary schools, but there are high schools with similar structures that require students to get internships to complement their in-class learning. In each case, parents and families are heavily involved at all levels of school functioning.

Because cooperative schools require a tremendous time commitment from parents, we most often find them in affluent neighborhoods where one parent does not have to work. They are also commonly found in rural areas where school choices are at a minimum. In Fall 2015, a group of community members and parents opened the doors of a new K–12 cooperative charter school in Anchorage, Alaska: P.A.I.D.E.I.A. Cooperative school.

P.A.I.D.E.I.A. stands for "Passionately Accommodating Individual Desires Enhancing Individual Achievement." They explain their school name as "from the Greek and means the whole training and education of children relating to the cultivation of mind and morals. It includes the training of the physical and mental faculties in such a way as to produce a broad, enlightened, and mature outlook harmoniously combined for the maximum cultural development of the student."

This name exemplifies the core tenets of humanism in its focus on individualized learning and personal development. The goal of the school is to help students pursue their extracurricular interests while also getting an academic experience that complements those interests. The school is a homeschool-based learning program with academic classes offered on a flexible schedule three days a week. Parents get syllabi from certified teachers, but do most work at home as their child's primary teacher.

Families are strongly encouraged to participate in Friday field trips. Most trips are nature excursions to local parks or wildlife refuges and are organized through partnerships with local organizations and schools, such as the University of Alaska, Fairbanks. Parents are expected to bring a picnic lunch for their family because "the social and emotional element of student development is a fundamental component of [our] field trips."

The Academic Policy Committee, the governing organization of the school, designs field trips such as neighborhood scavenger hunts and leaf walks. They also created Exploratory Mondays, which include rotations through Music, Art, and Japanese—enrichment opportunities that otherwise would not be available for homeschooled students. The school also works closely with high school-aged students who would like AP coursework or remedial support.

TAKEAWAYS

Humanistic learning is the last standing pedagogical framework that explicitly cultivates children's social and emotional development. It is an educational approach that prioritizes student choice and interest over a standardized curriculum and high scholastic achievement. For those reasons, it's a rare pedagogical model that many parents take issue with because of the seemingly lackadaisical nature of learning.

Though the structure of humanistic schools is indeed less rigid than traditional classrooms, it is also more empowering. Students in these schools are taught to advocate for themselves and not be afraid to pursue interests beyond the academic curriculum. The emphasis on community-building and strong social skill development appeals to families interested in educating the whole child.

But be forewarned. Humanistic schooling requires immense parental involvement. Even in a Waldorf school, parents are expected to participate in school governance, attend field trips, and provide academic support outside of school. This model of education is not a good fit for parents with full-time jobs or a lot of commitments beyond the family.

Humanism is also not a good fit for children who are outcome-oriented and invested in being the best. The noncompetitive nature of humanism makes it perfect for students who are interested in trying new things, even if they aren't necessarily good at them. Strong teacher-student and student-student relationships are at the core of humanistic learning, and therefore offer opportunities for children to enhance their social skills.

Critics of humanism say it's too "soft" to compete in the dog-eat-dog world of educational accountability. The emphasis on social sciences instead of core disciplines like science, math, and history are thought to create children with strong emotional intelligence but little academic intelligence. Though that is debatable, humanistic schools do not have the testing found in traditional schools, so it is difficult to measure how much students know.

But if your interest is not academic achievement but personal growth, humanism aligns well with your values. If there are no Waldorf schools in your area, look for schools with peer mediation programs instead of harsh discipline policies. There should be a lot of field trips and community service to help children practice the life skills they've learned in class. Finally, students should have a lot of choice in determining what, when, and how they want to learn.

REFERENCES

Combs, A. W. (1981). Humanistic education: Too tender for a tough world? *The Phi Delta Kappan*, 62(6), 446–449.

Patterson, C. H. (1977). *Foundations for a theory of instruction and educational psychology*. New York, NY: Harper & Row.

PAIDEIA Cooperative School. (2015). Retrieved from: http://www.akpaideia.org/

Vocabulary to Know

Associated Words/Phrases	Definition
Psychoanalysis	A method of therapy in which patients' subconscious thoughts become conscious; Founded by Sigmund Freud
Self-actualization	When someone reaches their emotional and cognitive potential
Hierarchy of needs	A theory about the order in which people fulfill their personal needs; Founded by Abraham Maslow
Client-centered therapy	A method of therapy in which patients direct and determine their course of action; Founded by Carl Rogers
Real self	A person's current state of being; Who they are in the moment
Self-concept	A person's overall belief about who they are and what they can do
Self-worth	How a person feels about themselves; An aspect of self-concept
Self-image	A person's beliefs about how they appear
Ideal self	Who a person wants to be
Whole child	Considering children's emotional and social well-being in addition to their physical and cognitive needs
Emotional intelligence	A person's ability to regulate, express, and interpret emotions
Self-regulated learning strategies	Behaviors such as organization, goal-setting, and environmental structuring that students use to achieve academic success
Growth mindset	The belief that intelligence can be increased with appropriate effort and challenge
Restorative justice	A method of conflict resolution focused on reconciliation between offenders and victims
Peer mediation	A method of conflict resolution in which peers problem-solve together
Skills-based learning	Pedagogy primarily focused on teaching concrete cognitive and behavioral skills instead of content
Community-based learning	Learning in which work with community organizations is tied to academic content
Individualized learning plan	A student-directed plan for academic achievement
Cooperative schools	Schools that are founded and governed by community members

Figure 8.2

Chapter Nine

Socioculturalism

School is where children should be challenged to understand people, places and things that are different from what they know and have experienced.

—Uncle and guardian of 4 children

OVERVIEW

Pedagogical Model: *Socioculturalism*
Origin: *Psychology*
Learning Goal: *Co-construction of knowledge*
Best for:
Ages: *11 and up*

> Kids who are: *Talkative; Social; Culturally or Linguistically diverse; Concerned with "why" and not "what"; Auditory processors; Experiencing ADD or ADHD*
> Parents who: *Can be involved in learning both daily and for long-term projects; Want their children to learn about issues of diversity and difference*

SOCIOCULTURALISM IN THEORY

Socioculturalism is not a word many people have heard before. Even within the realm of psychology, it is not nearly as common as Constructivism (Chapter 7) or Behaviorism (Chapter 10). And Jean Piaget is certainly more of a household name than is Lev Vygotsky, the father of socioculturalism.

Vygotsky is important however, because he offered the world of education a practical theory for how children learn. Contrary to Piaget, Vygotsky believed that learning leads to development. He observed that sometimes children were unable to do something on their own that they could do with the help of someone else. That made him think that learning doesn't always happen in isolation and that more learning could happen with assistance from others.

For example, new readers often struggle with keeping their place in a sentence (we call this "tracking"). But when a teacher, parent, or older sibling places a finger under each word as children read, they have no problem tracking. Eventually children learn to help themselves by placing their own finger under words. That tiny shift in what a child can do because someone helped is what Vygotsky called the *Zone of Proximal Development* (ZPD).

The ZPD is the distance between what someone can do on their own (*actual development*) and what someone can do with the help of a knowledgeable other (*potential development*). It is strange that it took until the 1970s for this idea to be theorized, because it is at the core of what happens in schools. Children go to school where a knowledgeable other (the teacher) "pulls" their learning along by guiding their thinking.

This happens with adults too. Complete the following problem by hand: 45 − 29. For many adults, the primary method would be to "borrow." But borrowing is certainly not the only way to solve this problem. You could group the numbers, use a number line, or draw 45 circles and cross out 29. Choosing to borrow doesn't mean you can't solve this problem another way. It just means you wouldn't have thought of those ways on your own.

Vygotsky proposed that when learners are exposed to new ways of thinking or doing, it hastens the development of cognitive processes still in formation. In other words, teaching me how to do math by grouping is likely to refine my ability to hold and manipulate information in working memory. Learning would therefore be leading to development.

As the theory picked up steam, Vygotsky and his students were challenged to explain *how* learning happened internally, not just how it was provoked externally. They began by explaining that because learning and development occur with the help of people around you, it is inherently a social process. Further, because the learner is not passively acquiring information but is an active participant, Vygotsky described learning as the co-construction of knowledge.

To co-construct knowledge, individuals from the same social environment share ideas and construct agreed upon beliefs and understandings (similar to social constructivism). The sharing of ideas can be explicit through direct conversation or be observational, where novices watch an expert do something and then tries to do it themselves. After what Vygtosky called *guided participation*, the novice and expert would discuss the content or activity and perhaps refine their previously held beliefs.

Crucial to this process are *psychological tools* such as language or visualization that help learners *internalize*—or make sense of—the new information for themselves. So while two people are sharing ideas and working together to create a common understanding of something, each person is also interpreting that information in a unique way that aligns with that person's cognitive abilities and prior experiences.

Here is an example. What do you call the thing with wheels you put items in while shopping at a store? If you're from the northeast region of the United States, you probably call it a shopping cart. If you're from the southeast, you may call it a buggy.

When moving from New York to North Carolina, you are likely to have a moment of confusion if while shopping someone asks you for a buggy. It might take you asking questions, or the stranger pointing to your shopping cart, for you to learn what a buggy is. Once you realize it, you might say "oh! A shopping cart? They are over there."

In that short exchange, you and the stranger have come to a shared understanding of what this item with wheels *does*, though you label it differently. These labels are based upon your individual use of language derived from your experiences in a specific social environment. So even though you know what a buggy is now, you are unlikely to call it that because, frankly, that's just not how *you* think of the thing with wheels you put items in while shopping.

This scenario highlights one of the key conclusions of sociocultural theory: knowledge is socially situated. What people believe is constrained by their social environment and their psychological tools. As one's social environment changes, so will one's understandings and use of information. Knowledge is therefore neither stagnant nor universal.

SOCIOCULTURALISM IN PRACTICE

Though a simple theory psychologically, it is a bit more difficult to transfer into schools. In fact, socioculturalism flies in the face of traditional pedagogical practices in which the teacher teaches and students learn. Because the learning objective of a sociocultural classroom is to co-construct knowledge, the roles of both teachers and students shift.

Teachers are members of the learning community. Sometimes they are experts and sometimes they are novices. Likewise, students bring their own experiences to the classroom and each has something unique to contribute to the learning process. The power dynamics in a sociocultural classroom are not hierarchical; the teacher is almost always on equal footing with students when it comes to learning new things.

But sociocultural schools are not democratic schools. Democratic schools are better aligned with humanistic learning because children in those schools are heavily involved in decision-making relating to their own learning. In sociocultural schools, children do not determine the *structure* of their learning, but rather participate in the construction of *what* they are learning.

It is therefore critical that the *classroom climate* is warm and supportive. For students to feel confident and courageous enough to share their ideas, they cannot be afraid of being wrong or embarrassed. Indeed, there is rarely a right or wrong in this classroom. Similar to social constructivist pedagogy, socioculturalism assesses students' ability to interrogate their own thinking.

Because the ultimate goal is the development of social knowledge, students must be able to identify why they believe something and how their beliefs are reflective of their upbringing and social environment. They must also be open to revising their beliefs in light of their classmates' different understandings of similar concepts.

Teachers must therefore design a learning environment that helps students develop the skills necessary to articulate their thoughts. The desks are organized in pods or a big circle to facilitate discussion through *dialogic/dialectic* teaching. Dialogic teaching methods are similar to the *Socratic Method* where questions are used to *scaffold* student thinking.

The ultimate goal of dialogism is that eventually everyone's thinking converges at a similar point of shared understanding. Dialogical teaching falls under the umbrella of *collaborative/cooperative learning*. True to sociocultural theory, collaborative learning involves students of varying ability levels working together toward a common goal. Students are responsible for one another's learning as well as their own, thus reinforcing the idea of community.

Students will almost always be working with a partner, in a small group or as a whole class, on assignments. It is also common for there to be stations through which students rotate, so everyone may not be working on the same subject matter at the same time. A good sociocultural teacher intentionally manipulates students' experiences to create *cognitive dissonance*, which forces students to be *metacognitive* about their learning.

The collaborative nature of the classroom facilitates teamwork skills. Students learn to navigate the nuances of working with others whose beliefs and abilities are different from their own. There is often explicit discussion about how to choose partners, assign roles, and determine a group leader. Students become adept at identifying the skills necessary to complete a certain task and the people best suited to do so.

Such detail-oriented thinking enhances students' analytical skills including problem-solving, reasoning, logic, and judgment. The intentional incorporation of diverse ideas and people forces students to synthesize information from multiple sources while also developing interpersonal social skills. Finally, at the core of these skills is the ability for students to be self-reflective and *self-reflexive*. Socioculturalism teaches children how to examine themselves as critical thinkers and social agents.

Most assessments in a sociocultural class will be reflective in nature. Students will be asked to walk through the evolution of their thinking by indicating how and why it may have changed. There is a lot of writing and projects, with fewer tests. If there are tests, they are likely to be short-answer or essay questions as opposed to multiple choice. Even on a math test, the desired outcome would not be the correct answer but, instead, a good explanation of the problem-solving involved in finding that answer.

It may seem like social constructivism and socioculturalism are very similar. That's because they are. If you think back to Chapter 7 and recall how constructivist theory became social constructivism, you will see why these two pedagogies are reminiscent of one another.

While the neo-Piagetians were altering Piaget's theory to include the concept of shared social knowledge, Vygotsky was already telling the world that social knowledge matters more than individual knowledge. In many ways, social constructivists piggybacked on Vygotsky's work to develop their theory.

But in practice these two theories do have differences. Most notably, the teacher's role and pedagogical practices are very different. Teachers in social constructivist classes guide students' thinking from afar. In a sociocultural classroom the teacher participates in the learning process. As a member of the learning community, the teacher has the difficult task of synthesizing everyone's diverse ideas so there can be consensus.

Social constructivist teachers are not aiming for group agreement. They simply want students to acknowledge and accept that different people believe different things. The discussion-based pedagogy in socioculturalism facilitates collective understandings whereas the project-based pedagogy in social constructivism facilitates individual understanding.

For whom socioculturalism is best. The advanced cognition involved in sociocultural learning can be difficult for children under age 8. Developmentally, they are not yet able to engage in metacognition, are still too egocentric to appreciate others' perspectives, and are motivated not by social cohesion, but by personal rewards and punishments. The goals and practices of socioculturalism are the opposite of young children's developmental capabilities.

Middle schoolers thrive in a sociocultural classroom. Their natural propensity for social interactions at this age makes socioculturalism an ideal pedagogical method. Kids' desire to impress their peers, coupled with their newfound independence and agency, provides them with the developmental skills to fully participate and appreciate a dynamic classroom. They also have the cognitive capacity to be reflective about their learning in an objective manner.

Personality wise, socioculturalism naturally appeals to social butterflies. The discussion-based teaching gives them a structured outlet for their chatter while also helping them learn to listen. Discussions are equally as good for introverts who have something to say but can't always find the space to interject their thoughts. But be aware of the difference between an introvert and a quiet child. If your child does not like to talk, socioculturalism is not a good fit.

Auditory processors will excel in this classroom where everything is pretty much oral. There are some kinesthetic experiences with projects, but very little visual stimulation. Because talking can happen much faster than reading and writing, children with processing deficits might struggle at first. They will likely need downtime to process through everything in a less hectic setting. Be sure to provide quiet time at home to allow them to decompress.

The fast pace of the sociocultural classroom appeals to students with ADD and ADHD. There are always new people talking, new places to go, and new ways to engage with learning materials. The constant bombardment of stimuli helps them stay focused and on task. Conversely, children who prefer a quiet work environment will have a hard time in this loud classroom. Many teachers require some quiet time, but these short intervals may not be enough for those who need silence to hear their own thoughts.

Socioculturalism is a good fit for a wide range of academic abilities. The ZPD accounts for all levels of learners and gives everyone an opportunity to shine. Each child will at some point be a novice and an expert, but will spend the majority of the time being pulled along by their peers. The lack of hierarchy and the absence of *ability grouping* make children less aware of learning deficits and more aware of their own academic strengths.

Finally, socioculturalism capitalizes on, and honors, difference. For *culturally and linguistically diverse* students, this classroom provides a space where being the "only" can be a positive experience. Far from singling students out, a good sociocultural teacher provides opportunities for all students to feel comfortable, knowledgeable, and capable. Different perspectives are welcome and appreciated.

A REAL LIFE EXAMPLE: COLLEGE PREP
IN OAKLAND, CALIFORNIA

College Prep is a private high school with an emphasis on collaborative learning through dialogical methods. Their website describes a mission statement that includes the creation of a "kind, creative, diverse, and joyful community" guided by 10 core beliefs:

1. We value the individuality of our community members and our egalitarian school culture.
2. We believe that high expectations, kindled curiosity, and dedicated effort encourage students to discern excellence and strive to do their best.
3. We affirm that deep learning requires patience, creativity, reflection, and practice.
4. We cultivate an awareness of self and others that is rooted in respect and empathy and emphasizes the importance of taking responsibility for one's impact and actions.
5. We work in a collaborative environment that gives young people opportunities to take risks, express themselves, and appreciate the perspectives and gifts of others.
6. We embrace the variety of backgrounds and life experiences within our community and recognize that the rich expression of diversity is essential to a meaningful education.
7. We integrate work and play, helping students recognize the elements of a balanced life.
8. We foster an understanding of interdependence and stewardship that starts with care for our open-air Oakland campus and extends to our greater community.
9. We prepare students to make a positive difference, encouraging engagement in a full array of school activities, and in service and learning opportunities in the broader world.
10. We dedicate ourselves, as teachers and mentors, to our own ongoing development, modeling commitment to learning and growth.

There are words that stand out in that list of core beliefs: community, egalitarian, reflection and practice, responsibility, interdependence, stewardship, diversity. These words highlight the sociocultural underpinnings of the school's academic and social culture. The heavy emphasis on translating academic learning into civic engagement underscores what Vygotsky believed the purpose of learning is: to become an active member of a social community.

The demographic composition of College Prep aligns with the pedagogical practices and goals of socioculturalism. The small class sizes of about 14 students ensure teachers can foster relationship with and between students. It also makes discussions, projects, and field trips more manageable than if there were 30 students in a single class.

The student body is approximately evenly split between female and male, and 57% of the students are students of color. The diverse student body ensures a good representation of ideas and perspectives which contribute to lively discussions and students learning how to understand and respect difference.

Another aspect of College Prep that is sociocultural is its governance structure. Students serve alongside faculty and staff on the Judicial Committee and the Curriculum Committee. The egalitarian governance is a good example of the guided practice that is critical to sociocultural theory.

They also have a week in spring during which students are encouraged to expand their learning beyond the school. With more than 40 options, students can participate in a variety of experiential learning activities around the city. The goal of this program is for students to not only apply their knowledge and skills, but to discover how other people may construct knowledge differently in different social environments.

Finally, College Prep has strong partnerships with community organizations where students do community service. But College Prep goes a step further and integrates students' work in the community into the academic curriculum, thus transforming community service into *community-based learning*. Helping students link their academic learning to the community encourages them to envision their learning as benefitting someone beyond themselves.

Assessment at College Prep includes traditional letter grades and qualitative feedback from classroom teachers. This feedback is based upon observation and personal interactions with individual students. True to sociocultural theory, College Prep teachers acknowledge that each student contributes uniquely to the learning community and thus requires individualized guidance. This process underscores the importance of personal relationships that facilitate communal, as opposed to individual, learning.

TAKEAWAYS

Socioculturalism encompasses many pedagogical techniques. There is small-group work, whole-class work, and individual work. There is a teacher floating around the classroom helping students as needed. There are discussions, field trips, essays, and projects. This is the type of educational experience most parents envision for their children.

Underlying the diversity of academic experiences are serious learning goals. A sociocultural classroom is designed with the intent to capitalize on students' developmental and personal strengths, so no two sociocultural classrooms will be the same. Similarly, the curriculum and assignments will shift from year to year as the teacher adjusts to meet the needs of current students.

The dynamic nature of a sociocultural learning environment requires a strong teacher with great content knowledge and good classroom management skills. A sociocultural teacher will be adept at facilitating discussion and comfortable talking about "hot topic" issues related to difference. Some of these issues (like sexuality and religion) may make you uncomfortable. But remember that while you may not always agree with what is being taught, trust that strong personal relationships go a long way to helping students access and interpret difficult material.

Just because you and the teacher may disagree from time to time about course content does not mean you are not welcome in the classroom. In fact, sociocultural classrooms should have heavy family involvement. As children's first teachers, parents and other family members are valued members of the learning community and are expected to contribute to students' educational experiences meaningfully and frequently.

Teachers may invite you to participate in school events, but more often you will be asked to extend your child's learning beyond the classroom. This may include fun family trips and might also involve helping with a community service project. What is unique about family engagement in socioculturalism is that it is continuous. Just as learning is a lifelong experience, children's projects and assignments are long-lasting.

You will therefore need to consider the extent to which you can actively participate in your child's schooling. Be prepared for daily homework help and long conversations about what happened at school. Remember that socioculturalism is about self-reflection, so you may not have to talk much, but you will have to listen and ask meaningful questions.

The younger your child is, the more they will need your help navigating this learning journey. Socioculturalists make it a point to make academic learning personal for students, so in many ways schooling becomes a highly emotional experience. Children under age 8 will not be able to take advantage of the learning opportunities provided by socioculturalism, but late elementary through high school students will do well in such a classroom.

Talkative children will learn when to speak and when to listen, and quiet children will not have to fight to be heard. High energy kids especially enjoy the fast pace of sociocultural learning, and deep thinkers like the challenge of integrating academic content with their social life. Students who struggled academically or socially can find a place in a sociocultural classroom that views all people as valuable members of the learning community.

Socioculturalism can be a great model for English language learners, sexual and racial minorities, immigrant children, and children with disabilities. Sociocultural teachers have great classroom management skills and an explicit desire to foster an inclusive learning environment. Their classrooms, teaching materials, and use of language should be representative and appreciative of diversity.

If your child is more interested in understanding why and how people think, rather than what they think, socioculturalism is a good fit. While College Prep is a private high school, there are many public schools in which collaborative learning and deep discussion are happening. Look for schools with long-standing community partnerships and strong family involvement programs. If there are required internships or community service hours, a school may be toying with sociocultural pedagogy.

REFERENCES

College Prep. (2015). Retrieved from: www.collegeprep.org
James, W. (1958). *Talks to teachers*. New York: Norton.
John-Steiner, V., and Mahn, H. (1996). Sociocultural approaches to learning and development: A Vygotskian approach. *Educational Psychologist*, 31(3/4), 191–206.
Koffka, K. (1921). *The growth of the mind*. London: Routledge and Kegan Paul.
Vygotsky, L. (1978). *Mind in society*. Cambridge, MA: Harvard University Press.

Vocabulary to Know

Associated Words/Phrases	Definition
Zone of Proximal Development (ZPD)	The difference between what someone can do alone and what someone can do with help
Actual development	What someone can do alone
Potential development	What someone can do with the help of a more knowledgeable person
Guided participation	When a novice/learner observes and practices a behavior with a more knowledgeable person
Psychological tools	Cognitive processes someone uses to make sense of new information
Internalization	When a learner makes sense of new information in the context of their own life and experiences
Classroom climate	The social and emotional "feel" of a classroom environment
Dialogic teaching	Using talk as the primary mode of teaching and learning
Socratic Method	A form of inquiry based on asking and answering questions
Scaffolding	Instruction that occurs step-by-step; Breaking a large process into small pieces
Collaborative learning	An instructional strategy in which small groups of students of varying academic levels work together to deepen their learning
Cognitive dissonance	When you have two or more conflicting thoughts or beliefs at once
Metacognition	Thinking about thinking
Self-reflexive	Thinking in which you reflect on changes in one's self as a result of a specific experience
Ability grouping	Grouping students based upon their prior or current academic performance level
Culturally and Linguistically Diverse (CLD)	Students whose beliefs, values, practices, and/or language differs from the White, middle-class, Christian, English standard
Community-based learning	Learning in which work with community organizations is tied to academic content

Figure 9.1

Chapter Ten

Behaviorism

You have to know the rules to play the game. Schools have to help kids learn how to be successful in today's society.

—Elementary School Principal

OVERVIEW

Pedagogical Model: *Behaviorism*
Origin: *Psychology*
Learning Goal: *Behavioral change*
Best for:
Ages: *8 and under*

> Kids who are: *Individual learners; Rule followers; Structured; Concerned with high grades; Extrinsically motivated; Experiencing processing-related learning disabilities; Experiencing ADD or ADHD*
> Parents who: *Do not have extra time or resources for cocurricular activities; Value good behavior and academic outcomes; Trust teachers to manage the educational process*

LEADING UP TO BEHAVIORISM

As is common in research, the order in which we discover things impacts the ways in which theories are formulated. Like many branches of psychology, behaviorism is borne of work conducted first on animals and then extended to humans. To understand human behavior in the late

1800s, psychologists like Sigmund Freud studied the human brain. But meanwhile, in the land of physiology...

Classical conditioning. The easiest way to remember *classical conditioning* is to remember Pavlov's dogs. Most people are familiar with the experiment in which Russian physiologist Ivan Pavlov trained dogs with a bell. In his study, Pavlov noticed that dogs salivate before food is even presented. He called food an unconditioned—or unlearned—stimulus. He called salivation an unconditioned response to the stimulus of food.

He then tried to see if he could reproduce the salivation response using a stimulus other than food. Turns out, when Pavlov presented food at the same time he rang a bell, after repeated exposure, the bell alone was enough to make dogs salivate. He called the bell the conditioned—or learned—stimulus.

The results of the study suggested that people can be trained at the subconscious level. All you have to do is pair something they naturally respond to with something you want them to respond to, and voila!

PSYCHOLOGICAL BEHAVIORISM

John Watson is considered the founding father of behaviorism, even though Pavlov set the stage for the emergence of the field in the late 1800s. By the early 1900s, Watson was sharing his ideas for a new approach to studying psychology that deviated sharply from the prior method of studying internal mental states.

Watson proposed that we focus on external, observable behaviors as indicators of internal processes. His idea was appealing because it was viewed as more scientific and more objective than collecting data that could not be evaluated by a standard rubric. In 1915, Watson was elected president of the American Psychological Association. Building on Pavlov's earlier experiment, in 1919–1920, Watson conducted his famous study on baby Albert and the white rat.

Similar to what Pavlov did with his dogs, Watson conditioned baby Albert to fear anything that resembled a white rat by clanging metal together every time Albert was given the rat. By the end of the experiment, Albert feared all furry items, including a Santa Clause mask. His study confirmed that, like dogs, humans could be conditioned to make mental associations between unrelated stimuli.

But humans are more complex than dogs, and it was thought that we should be able to learn in a more sophisticated manner than through simple stimulus response. In the 1930s, psychologist B. F. Skinner altered the work on classical conditioning by asking the question, how can we shape human behavior?

Operant conditioning. Similar to classical conditioning, *operant conditioning* is all about changing behavior. The difference here is that operant conditioning uses rewards and punishments. While these experiments were first done on rats in a maze, it is now a common parenting technique. It's not unusual to hear parents encouraging their children to do their homework if they want dessert after dinner.

Giving a child a reward in order to elicit a desired behavior is called *positive reinforcement.* If that same parent were to promise that there wouldn't be a bedtime, that would be *negative reinforcement.* It's still *reinforcement* because the parent wants the behavior of doing homework to increase. But it's negative because the parent is taking something away instead of giving something (which would be positive).

Similar methods are used when parents want a certain behavior to decrease. If your teenage daughter continues to break curfew, you might choose to *punish* that behavior after reminding her multiple times when she is expected home. Just like with reinforcement, you can punish a behavior both positively and negatively. *Positive punishment* involves giving a child something they don't want (chores), whereas *negative punishment* is when you take away something they do want (cell phone).

There are some caveats involved in this kind of parenting. First, in order for rewards and punishments to be effective, they need to be relevant to the specific child. For instance, if you reward your son with more TV time and he really prefers to spend his free time reading, then TV won't be enticing enough to make him change his behavior. The same is true for punishment. Putting kids in timeout only works if you have a child who dislikes being alone and quiet.

The second caveat is that operant conditioning requires intentional consideration of when you deliver rewards and punishments. In psychology we call this the *schedules of reinforcement.* If you want a behavior to change quickly, you need to reward or punish that behavior every time it happens, and to do so immediately.

If you don't mind slow change over time, you can reward or punish a behavior some of the time. The benefit of *continuous reinforcement* is that it's faster. The negative is that it is easily unlearned. *Partial reinforcement* takes longer but is more likely to engender long-term behavioral change.

EDUCATIONAL BEHAVIORISM

Behaviorism in schools looks very similar to behaviorism at home. Teachers use these techniques in the same ways as parents and for the same reason: to change students' behaviors. Because the emphasis in behaviorism is on behaviors, it is not a pedagogical model. It is instead a model of classroom management. Few teachers would call their class-room management methods "behaviorism," but all classrooms implement some element of reward and punishment.

Elementary schools use behaviorism most explicitly. This makes sense because the early period in children's educational journeys is when we want them to acquire appropriate learning behaviors. Some teachers use the color system where blue means you had an excellent day and red means you had a pretty bad day. Others use dots, stickers, or points you can cash in for a chance to reach into the treasure box on Friday.

No matter the method, the point is that teachers want students to not only behave properly but to be aware of their behaviors and how they affect others in the classroom. This remains true as children progress into middle and high school. Most junior high schools don't punish students by with-holding recess (negative punishment). Instead, students are given detention, parents are called, or apology letters are written (positive punishment).

Secondary students are also given fewer chances to fix their behavior than elementary students. It is expected that by 6th grade kids know the rules and have the self-regulatory skills to monitor and modify their behavior. The problem in most middle and high schools, however, is that behavior management is a school-level process. Individual teachers are no longer in control; instead, school and district policies become the faceless prosecutors of misbehavior.

This is problematic because policies cannot be enforced as consistently and immediately as necessary to be effective at changing students' behav-ior. Some teachers know policies inside-out and can spot misbehavior a mile away. Other teachers have never read discipline policies and use their own behavioral expectations as a guide. This also means that some teachers enforce harsh *zero tolerance* policies while others use a simple reprimand for the same behavior.

What it looks like in the classroom. Although behaviorism is mostly appli-cable in schools as a classroom management method, the tenets of behav-iorism form the foundation for many traditional pedagogical approaches. In fact, most public school classrooms operate within a behavioristic framework. The learning goal in such a classroom is to develop appropri-ate learning behaviors.

Behavioristic teachers provide structure by creating an environment that is free from distraction. They *scaffold* students' behaviors by giving rewards and punishments. The ultimate goal is for students to develop *self-regulatory learning strategies* so they can monitor their own behavior. The logic behind this approach is that if students are able to control their behavior, they will be better able to focus on the academic content.

To help limit distractions and children's natural desire to chit chat with friends, the desks are in straight rows and columns. Often, the teacher has assigned seats with a lot of intention: to break up friend groups, minimize conflict, or just to keep an eye on the class clown. The walls in a behaviorist classroom have a lot of posters outlining the rules and conveying positive messages about the importance of doing well in school.

An effective behaviorist teacher has clear expectations for academic work and social behavior. A behaviorist teacher might write a behavioral goal for the day on the board. The students would be reminded of the goal throughout the day and could end the day by sharing with the class if they thought they'd achieved the goal.

Common academic goals might be things like writing a complete sentence (elementary), using three vocabulary words (middle school), or writing a persuasive essay in Shakesperian dialect (high school). Behavioral goals might include raising hands before speaking, not texting during class, or completing a group project with classmates to whom you've never spoken.

Regardless of the specific goals, the work in a behaviorist classroom is almost always *teacher-directed*. Teacher-directed pedagogy is usually skills-oriented and involves the teacher explicitly telling the students what to do. In a science class, a behaviorist teacher would write the steps of the scientific method on the board, have students copy the steps, then demonstrate how to do each step. They may even watch a video of someone doing an experiment.

The students might then read a chapter in their textbook on the history of the scientific method before trying to repeat the steps on their own during lab time. Students' work is very procedural and will likely incorporate worksheets for practice. Content is very important, so traditional textbooks will form the core of academic learning materials. The rigid structure of textbooks aligns with the routine nature of behaviorism.

Behaviorist teachers rely heavily on tests to measure students' learning. Points are awarded if (a) the student followed all the appropriate steps and (b) got the correct answer. When students do not perform well, they are often offered an opportunity to revise their work and resubmit for half credit. This allows students to learn from their mistakes.

Standardized testing is the most commonly used behavioral teaching method. The word standardized underscores the tenets of behaviorist theory which states that everyone can and should perform the same way on the same task if their training was the same. This is why behaviorist teachers drill students with practice tests in preparation for the real test. The more practice students have taking a test, the better they should do on it.

Unlike in the other pedagogical approaches discussed in this book, behaviorist classrooms incorporate very little student agency. To ensure everyone is on the same task and learning the same content, students are not given a lot of choice in how or what they learn. The curriculum is adhered to closely and there is little space for creative projects and group learning. In accordance with behaviorist theory, the learning in a behaviorist classroom is individual.

The lack of creativity can be troubling for some parents, but the goal of a behavioristic classroom is not about difference, it is about sameness. The ultimate outcome is to equip students with the necessary skills to take charge of their learning and ensure they set themselves up for success long-term. In addition to hand-raising and note-taking, behaviorist teachers help students cultivate nuanced skills related to organization, planning, revision, and self-evaluation.

For whom behaviorism is best. Behaviorism is not developmentally appropriate for everyone. As a classroom management technique it is definitely most suited for children ages 8 and under who are generally motivated by the same things. As kids get older, they develop different interests and value different things in life. That makes it hard for teachers to find rewards and punishments that are applicable and effective for everyone in the classroom.

Morally, children under age 8 believe strongly in right and wrong. There is no gray area and intentions are not considered when they judge behavior. Behaviorism aligns with children's need to have a clear authority figure who determines what is good and what is bad. The consistency and explicitness of rules give young children a firm foundation for developing appropriate school behavior.

As a pedagogical approach, behaviorism remains most effective for children up to age 8, who are in the *preoperational* stage of cognitive development. These kids don't have the cognitive capacity to determine cause and effect, engage in problem-solving, or to reason about the future. They do better with the *instruct-solve* model of teaching because it provides time to slow down and practice a skill without being overly concerned with conceptual understanding.

This also means that children with a curious nature are not well suited for behaviorism. The focus is not on depth, so there will be little opportunity for students to immerse themselves in a topic of interest. Similarly, children who enjoy building things, drawing, acting out scenes, or just telling stories will not be able to indulge their creative side in a behaviorist classroom. Behaviorism is better for children who thrive within a strict schedule and consistent routines.

Personality-wise, behaviorism is great for kids who prefer to work alone or are naturally quiet by nature. That said, children need to be emotionally resilient and not easily embarrassed, because reprimands are public in behaviorism. Children who follow rules and don't mind being told what to do will excel under this model, especially if they are motivated by extrinsic forces like praise, treats, or the threat of punishment.

The emphasis on direct instruction in combination with heavy use of textbooks and worksheets makes behaviorism appealing for visual and auditory learners. If your child prefers reading and writing over speaking and doing, your child will be comfortable in a behaviorist class. Further, kids with strong test-taking skills will excel on the skill-based assessments.

Children who are less concerned about final grades and academic awards might struggle in this outcome-oriented model of schooling. Whereas a social constructivist teacher will praise students for the many ways they devised to solve a math problem, a behaviorist teacher will praise them for getting the right answer. If you are a parent who emphasizes the effort children put into their actions, your child may find it hard to transition into a classroom that doesn't acknowledge effort as much as the final product.

Because the goal of a behaviorist class is to equip everyone with the same knowledge and skills, the pacing of the class is determined by what the majority of the students need. This means that kids who are behind or ahead of learning goals will not get the individualized attention they need to do well in school. If your child is classified as gifted, you will want to look carefully at opportunities to work ahead, perhaps by using materials from higher grade levels.

Interestingly, the structure of behaviorism can work well for children with processing-related learning disabilities. The procedural nature of the instruction breaks skills and content into small pieces, thus helping students who may struggle with thinking about too much at once. The emphasis on practicing skills gives slower thinkers the time they need to truly grasp a concept before being asked to apply it.

Behaviorism may also be good for children with ADD or ADHD because it can help them learn self-regulatory behaviors. Many children with attention disorders have an overload of brain chemicals that makes it hard for them to focus. Behaviorism is all about training the brain and body to routinely engage in specific behaviors. This kind of structure can complement medications designed to help students develop cognitive and physical self-control.

Conversely, children with emotional disorders might find it difficult to be in such a strict learning environment. Unlike in humanism, there is little emphasis on the emotional well-being of students in a behaviorist class. If your child has any type of anxiety disorder, the constant threat of punishment may cause more anxiety. Even immense praise cannot counteract social embarrassment, especially in middle school when social issues are paramount.

Behaviorism is perhaps the pedagogical approach that aligns least with what parents want for their children. In our high-stakes era, parents want to combat the pressure placed on kids with a warm teacher and welcoming classroom environment. But not every child needs hugs and effusive praise to feel confident about their abilities. And not every child buckles under the pressure for high academic achievement.

The beauty of behaviorism is that it can be equally as effective for those whose personality pushes them to high achievement as it is for kids who lack academic initiative. Some children truly do learn better in a controlled environment with clear expectations and many opportunities for practice and immediate feedback. Remembering that educational decision-making is about the child, not the parent, might frame behaviorism in a more positive light.

A REAL LIFE EXAMPLE

We see behaviorist teaching methods most often in schools with less than stellar test scores. The teachers prioritize learning outcomes because in the current age of accountability there are high stakes associated with test scores.

Behaviorism is also common in under performing schools because statistically those are the schools with limited financial and personnel resources. Behaviorism does not require expensive teaching materials, nor does it require a small teacher-student ratio. It works well in schools with large class sizes because the emphasis is on behavioral control.

Perhaps the most commonly seen example of behaviorism in action is in military academies. We also see it in many college prep charter schools. The most expansive network of charter schools that employ behavioristic methods are the KIPP (Knowledge is Power Program) open-enrollment K-12 public schools. At present, KIPP includes 60 elementary schools, 80 middle schools, and 22 high schools nationwide.

KIPP academies are located primarily in under-resourced areas and enroll students through a lottery system. Most students who choose a KIPP school do so because their needs are not being met in their local public school. KIPP has a long-term goal of college graduation, a focus on character development, and an emphasis on family-school collaboration.

KIPP operates within a five-pillar framework: high expectations, choice and commitment, more time, power to lead, and a focus on results. Sound familiar? True to behaviorist theory, KIPP helps their students learn proper academic behaviors. The goal is to create a community of learners who are accountable for one another. They do this by stressing the importance of respect and responsibility.

Teachers at KIPP use the same curriculum as other public schools in their state. The difference is that KIPP teachers may alter the sequencing of lessons to accommodate the procedural nature of behaviorism. The curriculum spirals so that skills are slowly developed and built upon over time. Like other college prep schools, KIPP relies heavily on student data to assess learning and growth. In other words, as a behaviorist school, KIPP is outcome-oriented.

Indeed, their website is full of data citing their 45% 4-year college graduation rate, which is 11% higher than the national average. They also have impressive data about student growth where 50% of their students meet academic growth targets. The data on students' academic achievement is not as positive, but given that most students who attend a KIPP school arrive multiple grade levels behind, they have a long way to go before they are at the top of the class.

What KIPP continues to do well is teach students the behaviors necessary to facilitate optimal learning. Students at KIPP schools are motivated by rewards like parties, field trips, and uniform-free Fridays. There are strict punishments for misbehavior that range from social separation (seating a student alone in the class) to expulsion. The strict schedules and daily routines make the learning process predictable: which can be comforting for many children.

TAKEAWAYS

Behaviorism, when described in its true form, gets a bad reputation. People conjure up images of reform school or a juvenile detention center. The truth is that behaviorism *is* focused on rules and proper behavior, but not at the expense of learning content. In fact, the emphasis on rules, when done correctly, enhances learning.

Behavioristic pedagogy helps students engage with content in a deliberately structured fashion. While the pace is not always slow, the method of teaching leaves little room for confusion. Many people criticize direct instruction as being too linear and too rigid. While it is indeed rigid, it does not have negative effects on students' achievement.

On the contrary, many of the world's educational leaders have school systems structured around behavioristic teaching methods. For example, South Korea's Ministry of Education states that the aims of education are

> to improve basic abilities, skills and attitudes; to develop language ability and civic morality needed to live in society; to increase the spirit of cooperation; to foster basic arithmetic skills and scientific observation skills; and to promote the understanding of healthy life and the harmonious development of body and mind (South Korean Ministry of Education, 1996).

South Korea ranked 5th in the world for math and reading scores and 7th for science on the Programme for International Assessment in 2012 (*The Guardian*, 2013). The United States ranked 36th.

An emphasis on specific skills is more straightforward than relying on students to interpret content on their own. The assessment of skills is also easier and can provide more clarity about students' academic strengths and weaknesses. Many European countries (Germany, France, England) rely heavily on standardized assessments as early as 4th grade to determine if children will attend an academic or vocational high school.

The clarity of the curriculum means that instruction-based parental involvement is low. Rarely are parents asked to help students learn content. Instead, parents are asked to help their children practice skills. A teacher might send a student home with extra worksheets so they can rehearse the steps involved in long division or how to construct a paragraph. This means that while you do not need to be a content expert, you will need to be familiar with how the teacher wants students to engage their coursework.

There are minimal long-term projects or field trips in a behaviorist class. There won't be extra expenses or requests for chaperones; however, there might be requests that you reinforce school rules and academic expectations at home. Behaviorism works best when there is consistency across home and school.

Children who appreciate structure and prefer to work alone will find themselves at home in a behaviorist classroom. The behaviorist model of teaching focuses on learning behaviors in addition to academic content. Rewards and punishments are common, so extrinsically motivated children appreciate the opportunity to earn praise and sometimes special treats. While this model is best for children under the age of 8, older students who need more oversight can benefit too.

Look for a different type of school if your child is highly social, enjoys group work, or loves to express their creativity. They might feel stifled in a classroom with more traditional teaching methods. Similarly, children who like school because they are intellectually curious will likely not have that need satiated in a behaviorist classroom. But if your child is a straight shooter who is concerned about grades, a behaviorist school may be a good fit.

REFERENCES

Knowledge is Power Program. (2015). Retrieved from: www.kipp.org
South Korean Ministry of Education. (1996). Korean Educational Development Institute. *The Korean Education System: Background Report (Tentative Draft) to the OECD.*
The Guardian. (2013). Retrieved from: http://www.theguardian.com/news/datablog/2013/dec/03/pisa-results-country-best-reading-maths-science

Vocabulary to Know

Associated Words/Phrases	Definition
Classical conditioning	Learning involving associating a stimulus with a specific response
Operant conditioning	Learning involving rewards and punishments
Positive reinforcement	Giving something desired in an effort to increase a specific behavior
Negative reinforcement	Taking something undesirable away in an effort to increase a specific behavior
Reinforcement	The process involved when you want to increase a specific behavior
Punishment	The process involved when you want to decrease a specific behavior
Positive punishment	Giving something undesirable in an effort to decrease a specific behavior
Negative punishment	Taking something desirable away in an effort to decrease a specific behavior
Schedules of reinforcement	The rate at which a reward or punishment is received
Continuous reinforcement	Rewarding or punishing a behavior every time it is performed
Partial reinforcement	Rewarding or punishing a behavior sporadically
Zero tolerance	Discipline policy in public schools wherein suspension and expulsion are the first course of action when students misbehave
Scaffolding	Instruction that occurs step-by-step; Breaking a large process into small pieces
Self-regulatory learning	Learning where the student is actively participating in planning, goal-setting, help-seeking, and other learning behaviors
Teacher-directed	Instruction, usually skills-based, where the teacher explicitly tells students what to do
Preoperational	The second stage of Piaget's cognitive developmental theory
Instruct-solve	Similar to teacher-directed instruction. Instruction (usually math or science) where the teacher tells students what to do and then students practice

Figure 10.1

SUMMARY THOUGHTS

I hope it is clear that the choices teachers make are purposeful and theo-retically driven. Each model of learning has its own objective, unique role of the teacher, and particular instructional methods that support desired outcomes. How teachers measure student learning is largely dependent upon what it is they want children to know and be able to do.

No single learning goal is better than another, just as no method of learning is best. What's important to remember is that the overall goals, pedagogical practices, and assessment methods must align with your child's developmental abilities and social interests.

If you're looking at the chart below and realizing that your kid doesn't fit perfectly in any of the categories, that's okay. Fortunately, there is a hierarchy, so not everything should be weighted equally in educational decision-making.

For kids under age 10, the developmental appropriateness of a class-room matters most. Because young children have such varied cognitive abilities, and because their brains change so quickly, it is very important that learning objectives and instructional methods are carefully evaluated and reevaluated throughout the school year.

As wonderful as young kids are, they just are not able to do everything older children can do. Learning goals that involve complex thinking are a bit beyond the reach for elementary school students whose frontal lobes are just beginning to grow. Cognitive skills like reasoning, synthesis, and judgment can be very difficult for 8-year-olds. They just haven't had enough time and experiences for their brain to be able to process a lot of information in multiple ways.

What is appropriate for young children are classrooms that focus on practicing emerging cognitive skills. This practice should be hands-on and visual, and involve less auditory learning (which happens in the still-developing temporal lobe). Videos and activities should form the core of learning materials. Worksheets will help children rehearse important skills, but textbooks will not be effective for these new readers.

Humanistic and behaviorist classrooms both have elements beneficial for young children. This is ironic, given how different these two approaches are. In fact, it would not be an overstatement to say they are polar oppo-sites. While humanism is concerned with children's emotional well-being, behaviorism is focused on children's actions. The choice between the two comes down to differences in temperament and personality.

If your child is temperamentally anxious or sensitive, a humanistic class is optimal. But if your child has an easygoing temperament and is willing to work hard, a behaviorist class is a great choice. While young kids are cognitively and socially plastic, their temperament is not open to influence, so it's very important that you find a school aligned with their emotional disposition.

For children 10 and older, it's okay to prioritize the social appropriateness of schools. By age 8, our brains start to level out in terms of innate abilities. By 10 or 11, foundational cognitive skills are present, so the emphasis now is not on brain development but on refinement. Remember that synaptogenesis happens for the second time during puberty. While kids' brains are resetting, development shifts its focus from cognitive skills to social skills.

Once children enter middle school it is critical that their social environment stimulates the development of social skills such as communication, independence, and conflict resolution. They should also be in an environment that prompts them to explore the many aspects of their identity including racial and sexual identity. High schoolers should be thinking about their future selves and making a plan to achieve personal goals.

Pedagogical approaches like social constructivism and socioculturalism are good fits for adolescents because they capitalize on kids' social natures at this stage in development. The diverse type of feedback helps teens reflect on and adjust both academic and personal goals. The choice between social constructivism and socioculturalism really comes down to the way children learn best and if they prefer working alone or in groups.

The final and least important (sorry!) consideration is the level of parent involvement required in each model. Yes, children learn more if they have out-of-school support that helps them practice and extend what they are learning in school. But parental support is not the primary method through which children learn, and home is not the primary location of children's learning.

If you are forced to choose between a humanistic classroom that would be perfect for your child and a 60-hour-a-week work schedule, choose humanism. Developmentally appropriate schooling has a bigger influence on children's academic outcomes than does parent involvement. You may feel bad for being *that* parent in a Waldorf school, but take solace in the fact that you made the best choice for your child, not for you.

Table 10.1

	Constructivism	Humanism	Socioculturalism	Behaviorism
Learning Objective	Critical thinking	Growth	Co-construction of knowledge	Behavioral change
Teacher's Role	Guide	Supporter	Participant	Director
Instructional Methods	Project-based, Inquiry-based	Skills-based, Interdisciplinary	Community-based learning, Discussion-based	Direct instruction
Assessment Methods	Qualitative and Quantitative	Qualitative	Qualitative and Quantitative	Quantitative
Level of Parent Involvement	Moderate	High	High	Low
Ideal Age of Student	11+	All ages	11+	8 and under
Ideal Type of Student	Creative, Social, Inquisitive, Kinesthetic learner, Process-oriented, Gifted, Has a processing deficit	Shy, Self-motivated, Has diverse interests, Independent, Has a learning disability	Social, Team-oriented, Auditory learner, Has ADD or ADHD, Culturally or linguistically diverse	Likes to work alone, Extrinsically motivated, Likes structure, Outcome-oriented, Has ADD or ADHD

Chapter Eleven

Considerations for Culturally and Linguistically Diverse Students

We are here to teach all children regardless of SES, race, sexuality, gender, or nationality. We just haven't figured out how to do that well in our current system.

—School Superintendent

THE FAILURES OF PUBLIC SCHOOLS

Of the 51 million students in the US public school system, 24.5 million identify as a racial or ethnic minority, 4.4 million students are English language learners, and 26 million participate in the federal free and reduced lunch program.

Despite billions of federal monies earmarked for education reforms, students of color, English language learners, and low income students continue to have lower achievement levels than their white, middle class peers. In fact, math and reading scores for all *culturally and linguistically diverse* (CLD) groups were lower in 2015 than in 2013.

The *achievement gap* between 8th grade Hispanic and white students in 2015 was 21 points in reading and 22 points in math (on a 500 point scale). The gap between black and white students was similar: 26 points in reading and 32 points in math. There was a 45 point gap in reading scores, and a 38 point gap in math scores, between ELL students and students fluent in English. The gap between low income and higher income students was 24 points in reading and 28 points in math.

Decades of research confirm there is an obvious disconnect between the needs of diverse learners and what they receive in our current public school system.

Most CLD students attend urban schools that experience high teacher attrition rates and also have a disproportionate amount of unlicensed and novice teachers than schools in rural or suburban areas. Though data suggests that licensed teachers are more effective than unlicensed teachers, students most in need of experienced teachers are least likely to have them.

The unfortunate reality is that CLD students are often *double* or *triple minorities*. This means that they are members of multiple minority groups. In 2013, the wealth of white families was 10 times the wealth of Hispanic families and 13 times the wealth of black families. In other words, racial and ethnic minorities are more likely to be poor compared to whites.

If you add in the characteristic of language, many ELL students are nonwhite and living in poverty. As discussed in Chapter 6, being a racial or language minority can make school an unwelcome and difficult place to be. From the curriculum to pedagogy to school policies, parents of children whose identities mark them as "different" should pay close attention to how schools and teachers educate culturally and linguistically diverse students.

WHAT DOESN'T WORK

Jean Anyon, Martin Haberman, and Lisa Delpit dedicated their careers to researching differences in the quality of education diverse students receive compared to middle and upper income white students. Spanning four decades, their work (along with the work of many other scholars) has redefined what it means to be a good teacher.

Anyon's famous piece, *Social Class and the Hidden Curriculum of Work*, was published in 1980 but is still relevant today. She spent a year observing different classrooms to figure out what happens in schools serving particular demographics of students. She found that classrooms across *socioeconomic (SES)* levels had different learning goals and corresponding instructional practices.

Children who attended working class schools were taught to follow directions. Their work involved copying things down and completing worksheets—often in complete silence. Children in middle class schools were taught to get right answers. Most of their work came from the textbook and involved little creativity. Upper income children were assessed on their ability to be creative and demonstrate leadership skills. Their learning was *student-centered* and largely *project-based*.

In her analysis she discussed how each SES group was being taught different skills that would prepare them for vastly different jobs. Because of the routine nature of work in working class schools, children are being taught how to be laborers. In those positions, they would be successful if they complete tasks and follow rules.

Middle class students were being prepared for bureaucratic jobs like secretaries or managers. Their primarily role would be supportive and their work, procedural. Success in these positions, like in their classroom, is in finding the correct answer and solving problems efficiently.

Children in affluent schools were being taught to obtain professional positions like lawyer, accountant, or business executive. The agency and originality that was prioritized in school will be what makes them successful employers of others.

This research is important because it helps clarify how seemingly small things that happen in classrooms can, over time, track students onto particular life paths. All parents want their children to have more than they have, and education is often the way children become *socially mobile*. But too often children from low income families, in particular, are forced to attend schools that prioritize behavioral control over cognitive development.

If Anyon told us what happens in schools, Haberman's work took a step back to determine the context in which learning occurs. His work, *The Pedagogy of Poverty Versus Good Teaching*, describes the overarching framework under which schools serving low income students operate. His qualitative findings suggest that urban schools in particular have policies and procedures that communicate low expectations for both teachers and students.

In particular, he identifies four principles guiding urban education:

1. Teaching is the job of teachers. Learning is the job of students.
2. Teachers are in charge. Students should obey teachers.
3. Ranking students is inevitable because they have different abilities.
4. Children must learn basic life skills before they can learn academic content.

Under this paradigm, teachers are merely record keepers and task masters. They give information, ask questions, review information, assign work, grade work, monitor behavior, and punish misbehavior. These alleged pedagogical practices are similar to what Anyon describes in working class schools. Learning in these contexts is passive, not active.

Lisa Delpit's work finishes the tale of learning in diverse schools by describing why learning often fails to happen in classrooms where many students are not part of the racial or income majority. Delpit has published widely about how diverse students cannot fully receive the benefits of their education because they are not a part of the *culture of power*.

The culture of power includes both a group of people who get to determine rules and the rules that are decided upon by those in power. In schools, the culture of power is reflected in policies related to dress code, attendance, and behavior. Power is also reflected in the curriculum and teaching methods.

Those in power can be governmental bodies or they can be real-life people in the school. For example, the public school system is indeed a system with a history that defines the purpose of schooling. But that purpose is translated by real-life people in schools, such as superintendents, principals, school counselors, and teachers. Whatever beliefs those people possess are the norms and values you will see represented in schools.

Delpit highlights language as the primary way in which diverse students are excluded from educational opportunities. She discusses language as having many codes or rules. We all speak differently depending upon to whom we are speaking, where we are speaking, and what we are speaking about. Delpit's point is that the rules governing these decisions are determined by those who are in charge of the space and the content.

In classrooms, teachers get to decide what is talked about, when, and to whom. Most importantly, teachers get to decide *how* students should talk about certain things. Delpit's research suggests that diverse students don't automatically know when to use academic language and when to use slang. They also have a hard time determining which words count as academic and which words are slang.

When students' communication—both verbal and physical—are not aligned with teachers' cultural expectations, they are often considered misbehaved, rude, or ignorant. Delpit argues that in order for diverse students to be fully included in learning processes, teachers must explicitly explain the norms of the culture of power and invite students to participate in it.

WHAT WORKS

What does work in schools and classrooms with diverse students is something called *culturally relevant/responsive teaching/pedagogy* (CRT/P). CRT/P is an instructional method advocated for use with diverse students. Gloria Ladson-Billings (1995) listed three tenets of CRT/P: academic success, cultural competence, and sociopolitical awareness. Through strong teacher-student relationships, Ladson-Billings argues that teachers can make learning an empowering experience for diverse students.

Geneva Gay (2000) describes CRT/P as: "using the cultural knowledge, prior experiences, frames of reference, and performance styles of ethnically diverse students to make learning encounters more relevant to and effective for them" (p. 29). Such engaging curriculum and pedagogical approaches, when delivered by a *warm demander* who emphasizes positive relationships, increase the academic achievement of black, Hispanic, and low income students.

Why it works. Culturally relevant/responsive teaching/pedagogy is effective because it helps students see themselves in the curriculum. The connection of academic content to real life makes learning more meaningful.

CRT/P structures education as a communal activity, much like socioculturalism. Many diverse students are from cultural backgrounds that are more *collectivist* than individualistic. CRT/P is therefore more aligned with students' cultural norms and expectations for social interaction. Diverse students enter class as members of the culture of power instead of a threat to the culture of power.

Finally, the warm demander classroom management approach is reminiscent of many of the relationships diverse students have with adults in their own lives. High expectations, respect, and nurturing are at the core of strong personal bonds. When diverse students have such a relationship with their teacher, they feel safe and comfortable in their classroom.

WHAT YOU SHOULD DO

It can be difficult to "see" CRT/P without extensive investigation of a school. The first thing you should do is look up the schools' demographics. It is more likely that schools with diverse student and teacher populations are using CRT/P than schools with more homogenous populations.

Next, you should visit the school and talk to administrators. It's okay to be completely honest about concerns you have about your child's comfort and emotional safety. Request a list of school policies and an overview of the curriculum so you can see if the school is walking the walk and not just talking the talk.

Most important is for you to observe the classroom(s) your child is most likely to be in. If at all possible, schedule time to meet with future teachers. Bring a list of questions about their instructional methods, their prior teaching experiences, and the type of teacher preparation program they attended. If the teacher has a *CLD endorsement*, even better! This means they have extensive experience learning about and teaching diverse students.

On your way out of the school, pay attention to the decorations on the walls and in the office. What kinds of student work are displayed? Is it clear that all students' work is up or just a few samples of the best work? Are posters using inclusive language and diverse images or are they *hegemonic* in nature?

Be sure to pick up a copy of the school calendar of events. This will tell you what holidays the school celebrates and, more importantly, how they celebrate them. Most public schools adopt a *feasts and fiestas* approach to celebrating diversity.

This means that certain months, weeks, or days are dedicated to in-depth exploration of a particular demographic group. The problem is that those are the only times students learn about diverse people. Potlucks and costume parties are not appropriate ways to honor the contributions of marginalized groups.

The last thing you should do is review the school's test scores for the prior academic year. By law, the school is required to make this information available either in person at the school office or online. Don't just look at the overall scores; instead, look at the scores for specific groups of students. Just because the average scores are high does not mean the scores of ELL students, special education students, or ethnic minority students are also high. This information can tell you a lot about how well the school provides an *equitable* education.

TAKEAWAYS

The increasing diversity of public schools means it is imperative that we get better at meeting the educational needs of all students. Historically we've had a difficult time making sure that racial and ethnic minorities, ELL students, immigrant students, special education students, LGBTQIA students, and low income students are given what they need to succeed in school.

Many marginalized students are concentrated in the same schools, often in urban areas, where most of their teachers are unlicensed and/or new to the profession. Schools serving low income children in particular often use instructional methods that perpetuate class and cultural differences. The unequal distributions of resources and *deficit-based* teaching are, in part, what creates achievement gaps between underrepresented students and majority students.

Schools with high achieving CLD students have teachers with high expectations and good relationships with students and families. These teachers often use elements of culturally relevant/responsive teaching/pedagogy which ensures that the classroom climate, curriculum, and pedagogical practices are inclusive of all demographic groups.

Finding these schools is an extra task for parents of diverse students. In addition to being developmentally appropriate, K-12 classrooms must be places where children feel welcome and respected. It is almost impossible for healthy development to occur if children are not given the opportunity to embrace who they are.

You can identify good schools for diverse children by first looking at the demographics of the school population. When there are diverse students, teachers, and administrators, it is more likely that the school will endorse inclusive educational methods. Further, teachers with CLD endorsements on their teaching license are generally well prepared to teach diverse students. Finally, looking at school achievement data can tell you just how good a job a school is doing at educating all children.

REFERENCES

Anyon, J. (1980). Social class and the hidden curriculum of work. *Journal of Education*, 62(1), 67–90.

Boyd, D., Lankford, H., Loeb, S., and Wyckoff, J. (2005). Explaining the short careers of high-achieving teachers in schools with low-performing students. *American Economic Review*, 166–171.

Delpit, L. (1988). The silenced dialogue: Power and pedagogy in educating other people's children. *Harvard Educational Review*, 58(3), 280–299.

Gay, G. (2000). *Culturally responsive teaching: Theory, research, and practice.* New York: Teachers College Press.

Haberman, M. (1991). The pedagogy of poverty versus good teaching. *Phi Delta Kappan*, 73(4), 290–294.

Irvine, J. J. (1990). *Black students and school failure.* Westport, CT: Greenwood.

——. (2003). *Educating teachers for a diverse society: Seeing with the cultural eye.* New York: Teachers College Press.

Ladson-Billings, G. (1995). Toward a theory of culturally relevant pedagogy. *American Education Research Journal*, 32(3), 491–564.

——. (2009). *The dreamkeepers, successful teachers of African American children.* (2nd ed.). New York: Jossey-Bass

Pew Research Center (2014). America's wealth gap between middle-income and upper-income families is widest on record. Retrieved from: http://www.pewresearch.org/fact-tank/2014/12/12/racial-wealth-gaps-great-recession/

U.S. Department of Education. (2013). National Center for Education Statistics. *The Condition of Education.* Retrieved from: http://nces.ed.gov/programs/coe/indicator_cge.asp

——. (2014). Office of Special Education Programs. *Individuals with Disabilities Education Act (IDEA) database.* Retrieved from: https://inventory.data.gov/dataset/8715a3e8-bf48-4eef-9deb-fd9bb76a196e/resource/a68a23f3-3981-47db-ac75-98a167b65259

———. (2015). Institute of Education Sciences, National Center for Education Statistics, National Assessment of Educational Progress (NAEP), various years, 1990–2015 Mathematics Assessments. Retrieved from: http://www.nationsreportcard.gov

———. (2015). Institute of Education Sciences, National Center for Education Statistics, National Assessment of Educational Progress (NAEP), various years, 1992–2015 Reading Assessments. Retrieved from: http://www.nationsreportcard.gov

Ware, F. (2006). Warm demander pedagogy: Culturally responsive teaching that supports a culture of achievement for African American students. *Urban Education*, 41(4), 427–456.

Vocabulary to Know

Associated Words/Phrases	Definition
Culturally and Linguistically Diverse (CLD)	Students whose beliefs, values, practices, and/or language differs from the White, middle-class, Christian, English standard
Achievement gap	The difference in standardized test scores between genders and racial and economic groups
Double/Triple minority	When someone identifies as a member of more than one marginalized group
Socioeconomic status (SES)	Someone's economic and social position in relation to others based upon income, education and occupation
Student-centered	Instructional practices that prioritize the needs and desires of students
Project-based learning	Interdisciplinary instructional approach in which students investigate real-world problems over extended periods of time
Social mobility	The movement of people between economic and social positions
Culture of power	Those who define common norms, practices and values; the norms, practices, and values that are deemed normal
Culturally relevant/responsive teaching/pedagogy (CRT/P)	An inclusive instructional method that connects academic content to students' out-of-school lives
Warm demander	A teacher who has high expectations, is authoritative and nurturing
Collectivism	Societal norms, practices and values that prioritize the good of society over the individual
CLD endorsement	An additional certification teachers can earn if they undergo additional training on how to teach diverse students
Hegemonic	The dominant people or ideologies in a particular social environment
Feasts and fiestas	A phrase to describe the common ways in which schools celebrate diversity (i.e. through pot lucks and parties)
Equity	Giving each child what they need individually
Deficit-based teaching	Teaching that assumes children lack desired knowledge or skills

Figure 11.1

Conclusion

This book is not the end all end all, be all for educational decision-making. It is meant to help you through what is likely one of the most difficult decisions a parent can make. The schools children attend are not only where they spend the majority of their time, but also where they grow into the people they will become.

Yes, parents and families have a large influence on shaping kids' development, but in reality, much of what happens at home loses its impact once kids start school. School is where they learn the basic skills that facilitate all learning to come. School is where they meet their first best friend and develop the social skills to navigate that relationship. School is where they go all day, every day and have experiences that you can't control.

Entrusting your children into the care of somewhat complete strangers is terrifying, but there's not much you can do to avoid the day when you have to place your child's hand into the hand of their new teacher. Many parents identify that moment as a milestone when child rearing becomes a shared responsibility between the family and the school.

But even though school is where most learning happens, what you do for your child's education is equally as important to their learning as what goes on in their classroom. And that is completely up to you.

You decide where your child attends school and the types of children with whom they attend school. You decide the content they learn and the way in which they learn it. These decisions are what determine the educational experiences that will dictate children's future academic, professional, and personal opportunities.

The implications of your decisions are vast. For that reason, you can't send your children to any old school simply because it is close or familiar.

Decisions about children's schooling must be made in the context of their current and future developmental capabilities. What children can do simultaneously limits and expands educational possibilities.

The younger a child is, the more adaptable the child is to different types of classrooms, but the more often the child's needs change. Kids under age 10 need schools that prioritize their cognitive development. They need classrooms that teach them the basics of what it means to be a student and what it means to learn. The pedagogy they receive should be largely visual and hands-on, because those are the parts of their brain that are almost fully developed.

Once children begin middle school, all bets are off. As their brain reorganizes itself, preteens are more concerned about cultivating a social identity than an academic one. Your job is to find them a school that facilitates the exploration of identity in a safe and nurturing environment. What matters most to early adolescents is that the ways they view themselves are reflected and honored in school practices.

By the time they reach high school, they will know who they are and have ideas about what they want to accomplish. As hard as it is, you have to let go and trust that all of their prior experiences will help them make good decisions about their academic and social behavior. The most you can do is ensure they attend a school with the course offerings that reflect their interests, talents, and future goals.

And that's it. Where they go to college, if they go to college, what they major in, or if they design their own major, is completely up to them. Though you may not always agree with their choices, take comfort in the fact that you've spent 13 years modeling how to make developmentally and personally appropriate educational choices. That's the best you can do.